# ALONE TOGETHER

# ALONE TOGETHER

## Social Order on an Urban Beach

## Robert B. Edgerton

UNIVERSITY OF CALIFORNIA PRESS

BERKELEY · LOS ANGELES · LONDON

University of California Press
Berkeley and Los Angeles, California
University of California Press, Ltd.
London, England
© 1979 by
The Regents of the University of California
ISBN 0-520-03783-3
Library of Congress Catalog Card Number: 78-59448

1  2  3  4  5  6  7  8  9

# Contents

# Preface

To respect the privacy of persons who use it, the actual identity of "Southland Beach" has been disguised. The police force of "Southland City" shares in this anonymity, but it must be emphasized that no member of that police department asked for this protection. Their help and cooperation is gratefully acknowledged here, as is the cooperation of the many Los Angeles County lifeguards who generously gave their time after working hours. Because this lifeguard organization serves a much larger beach area than Southland Beach, there was no need to disguise its identity.

I am also indebted to several students who volunteered to assist with this research, most particularly to Geri-Ann Galanti, Rod Clark, and Wally McCall. To Cecile Mairesse, L. L. Langness, and many students in my graduate seminars at UCLA, I owe my thanks for commenting on earlier drafts of this manuscript. Lupe Montano, Jae Stewart, and Carmen Gateman typed various drafts of this book with skill and good humor; they also corrected many of my errors as they went along. This research was supported in part by the University of California and Grant No. HD-04612, Neuropsychiatric Institute, University of California, Los Angeles.
I owe a great debt to Lorel Cornman and Patti S.

Hartmann, my research associates. They contributed to this book not only through their many research activities—such as interviewing lifeguards, police officers, and beachgoers, and observing beach behavior—but also through their constructive criticism of all that is reported here. I am also extremely grateful to Don R. Sutherland for taking all of the photographs for this book.

# The Problem of Social Order on an Urban Beach

Beaches in Southern California attract millions of people; as many as a million visitors have been counted on a single summer day. This book will examine one of these beaches, which we shall call Southland Beach. Along with palm trees and orange groves, "the beach" is an integral part of the culture and mystique of Southern California. The beach in Southern California has an idyllic image, constructed out of the romantic memories of many men and women who spent a large part of their youth there, tanning themselves, body surfing, drinking beer, eating, and having fun in a supremely sensuous world of tanned young bodies in bathing suits. Many romances blossomed on the beach, not only between beachgoers, but between beachgoers and the beach itself. "Beach people"—local residents who loved the beach, went to it as often as possible, and thought of it as their own— became a distinctive part of Southern California life.

Like the orange groves, now mostly replaced by tract housing, the beaches that were once occupied primarily by "beach people" are becoming a memory too, even though movies and television continue to portray the earlier, romantic image of the beach. "Gidget" and "Beach Blanket Bingo" are strictly period pieces. Today millions of people from all over South-

ern California go to the beach. Most come from many miles
inland on the network of freeways that criss-crosses Southern
California. With the coming of these millions of people, many
beaches have been transformed. They are now urban places,
almost as diversely peopled as the vast urban sprawl that
surrounds them. Southland Beach is such an urban beach.
Because of its location, its ready access by freeway, and the
availability of public parking, it has probably attracted a
greater diversity of people from all walks of urban life than
any other beach in Southern California.

This book examines what these many and diverse people
do that enables them to get along together when they go to
the beach. It attempts to determine what they find enjoyable
and how they avoid trouble. More specifically, it is concerned
with how it is possible for these many thousands of strangers
of all ages and ethnic groups to come to a strip of sand,
remove almost all of their clothing, spend a day in close
proximity to one another, often drink alcohol and smoke
marijuana, and yet manage to avoid conflict with one another. The book asks what kind of social order exists at the
beach and how this order is achieved.

### The Problem of Order

To begin, let us consider the idea of social order. How is it
that human beings manage to get along together? Social scientists continue to be fascinated and perplexed by this; it is
perhaps their most fundamental question. Since Hobbes and
Locke in the seventeenth century, there has been an outpour-
ing of answers, variously attributing the orderly nature of
social life to tradition, social contract, human nature, law,
shared values, the definition of the situation, social equilibrium, and many other factors.[1] Sociologists such as Durkheim and Parsons, who focused on the problem of order at a
societal level, not surprisingly found the sources of order in
society itself. The resulting so-called functionalist view,
which until recently was so widely accepted that it has been
referred to as "the conventional wisdom" (Wrong 1961), assumed that people want to get along with one another be-

cause they internalize the values of their culture and because they seek the esteem of their fellows. But as functionalism and its equilibrium assumptions weakened, other theories began challenging for acceptance. Many of these challenging points of view shifted the focus of study from society as a whole to smaller social segments such as settings, occasions, situations, roles, scenes, episodes, and the like. In this latter tradition, we would particularly note the work of contemporary scholars such as Garfinkel and Goffman, while tracing their interests back to Weber, Simmel, Mead, Thomas, and Schutz.[2]

Whether the problem of order is approached at the macroscopic level of society itself or in some more microscopic way, there can be no doubt of one thing: the sources of social order are no longer widely agreed to be self-evident. The conventional wisdom of a decade ago has fragmented into a number of opposing positions. Unreconstructed functionalists remain, but their ideas are amended or disputed by conflict theorists, exchange theorists, control theorists, and systems theorists as well as by those who focus on symbolic or strategic interaction, or who practice ethnomethodology. The resulting ferment has opened new lines of inquiry into the perennial problem of order, even though no new consensus has yet emerged.

This study of Southland Beach draws upon developments in most of these fields, particularly from naturalistic studies of social deviance, from cross-cultural research on conflict, disputes, and law, and from the study of public behavior in urban settings.[3] It proceeds on the assumption that although there has as yet been no agreement about the conditions that allow people to get along with one another, that the *failure* of people to do so can be observed in the presence of conflict, dispute, criticism, outrage, disagreement, punitive retaliation or other kinds of behavior which can be referred to as "trouble." The occurrence of trouble, then, is not only a social problem; it also provides a means of understanding social order itself. Therefore, we study the frequency and seriousness of trouble. We do not assume that social order exists only when trouble is absent; on the contrary, we assume that some kinds of trouble will occur whenever human beings deal with one another (Edgerton 1976). But we do assume that orderly relations between human beings will break down if trouble becomes too frequent or too serious. We ask why that does not happen at Southland Beach.

### Trouble on the Beach

If one is interested in trouble as an index of social order, it might be asked, why study a beach? Consider the very puzzlement expressed in the question itself. A beach is a place for fun, not trouble. This belief is part of our cultural heritage, and it is reaffirmed by the people who go to Southland Beach. Thus it may be useful to pose the following deceptively simple question: How is it that so very many different sorts of strangers on this beach manage to get along together? Our belief that a day at the beach will be enjoyable and safe is so ingrained that we must almost force ourselves to ask why matters should, or even *could*, be otherwise. Why should one seriously entertain the idea that an urban beach could be an unpleasant and dangerous place, one where trouble occurs? The search for an answer begins by recalling that our cities themselves are undoubtedly troubled places, with many of their locations and activities being seen by all concerned as neither safe nor pleasant; and Southland Beach is near Los Angeles, one of the largest cities in the United States.

Many analysts of American society have noted that most of us no longer feel very happy or very safe in our cities. In his book, *The Pursuit of Loneliness: American Culture at the Breaking Point* (1970), Philip Slater provides an example of this line of thought. Slater believes that rampant individualism, which is most extreme in urban living, has left us 'disconnected, bored, lonely, unprotected, unnecessary, and unsafe" (1970:26). The United States President's Commission on Law Enforcement and the Administration of Justice (1967:v) concluded: "One-third of a representative sample of all Americans say it is unsafe to walk alone at night in their neighborhoods. Slightly more than one-third say they keep firearms in

the house for protection against criminals. Twenty-eight percent say they keep watchdogs for the same reason." The
Commission also reported that in high-crime districts sur-
veyed in Boston and Chicago, the fear of crime was such that
43 percent reported that they stayed off the streets at nights
and 35 percent said that they no longer spoke to strangers
(1967:50–51).

These concerns and fears are by no means recent phenomena. For example, New York's Central Park was reported
to be unsafe at night as early as 1872, and most American cities reported "crime waves" before the turn of the
century (Bettman 1974). However bad the conditions were a
century ago, it seems to be commonly agreed that they are
getting progressively worse. For example, in 1978 a Con-
gressional Committee reported that fully one-half of all
Americans were afraid to go out at night (*Los Angeles
Herald-Examiner*, January 9, 1978). And contemporary writers
continue to note with alarm the rise in such "urban problems" as crime, alcoholism, mental illness, suicide, aliena-
tion, and rape. The attention of many social scientists has
been focused on urban problems such as these, sometimes in
the hope that thereby the wellsprings of social order would be
discovered. While this hope has yet to be realized, many of
the facts of life in American cities are undeniably unpleasant.
People in cities do make trouble for one another all too frequently for the comfort of most of us, and Southland Beach
has become a part of a very large city.

Louis Wirth wrote a landmark article in 1938 entitled "Urbanism as a Way of Life," which stated, or understated, the
essence of city life in a way that still bears reflection: "The
close living together and working together of individuals who
have no sentimental and emotional ties foster a spirit of competition, aggrandizement, and mutual exploitation. To coun-
teract irresponsibility and potential disorder, formal controls
tend to be resorted to. Without rigid adherence to predictable
routines a large compact society would scarcely be able to
maintain itself. The clock and the traffic signal are symbolic of
the basis of our social order in the urban world" (Wirth

1938:15–16). Wirth asserted that human experience in cities is a product of three fundamental conditions: (1) large numbers of people, (2) who are socially heterogeneous, and, (3) densely packed together.

Many since Wirth have agreed that what we see as prototypically urban—including urban "trouble"—is a product of these three features (Milgram 1970). Others, basing their conclusions on a long history of urban research, have linked urban troubles not only to large numbers and to diversity, but to the social uncertainty that exists between strangers in a metropolis. Wirth himself, for example, believed that city life would be impossible without mechanical routines that would guide city dwellers through an uncertain and diverse city environment. That uncertainty and diversity can lead to trouble among people has been noted by many, from anthropologist Mary Douglas (1966) to sociologist Robert Scott (1972:21), whose following opinion has been widely echoed: "Uncertainty and diversity are the natural enemies of order because they are potentially more powerful than the order that stands against them."

Southland Beach is characterized by all of these conditions: large numbers, density, social heterogeneity, and uncertainty. Lifeguards' estimates of the number of people who visit the beach run from 12 to 16 million annually, and most of these come during the summer; during the two hottest months—July and August—anywhere from 6 to 9 million people come to a strip of sand slightly less than three miles long and 100 to 200 yards deep, comprising 153 acres.

On the most crowded days when as many as 400,000 beachgoers are on Southland Beach, almost all available sand is occupied. Even an average summer crowd of 100,000 means that there is more than one person per 100 square feet. Such density is possible because some beachgoers leave during the day to be replaced by others, and because many beachgoers come to the beach in groups, and crowd together with as many as seven to ten other people within 100 square feet of sand.

The people who visit Southland Beach are socially heterogeneous. While there are some areas of the beach that attract primarily young "middle-class" whites, most beach areas are diversely populated by young and old, both men and women, by people of varying occupations and income levels, and by persons from a variety of ethnic groups. While we can offer no precise demographic proof, it appears to us, as it does to lifeguards, police officers, and many beachgoers, that Southland Beach attracts a population almost as diverse as that found in the larger Los Angeles metropolitan area. So great has this diversity become, that many lifeguards and beachgoers refer to Southland Beach as a "melting pot" for all of Los Angeles—despite the fact that most beachgoers have little to do with one another. The diversity is so great that on most parts of the beach it would be impossible on any given day to predict what one's "neighbors" at the beach might be like—young or old, alone or in a family group, black or white, English-speaking or not. Not only are beachgoers heterogeneous, but, by our observations and their own admission, they remain strangers to one another. They keep to themselves or stay with the group they came with.

Southland Beach, then, is densely crowded by all sorts of strangers. This alone should provide the potential for misunderstanding and conflict, but there are additional aspects of beachgoing that make trouble even more likely. As in no other public place, people at the beach undress, and most beachgoers wear skimpy bathing suits throughout their stay at the beach. Not only is everything that one does visible to hundreds of strangers, but almost all of one's body is also visible. Also, many beachgoers drink alcohol, smoke marijuana, or take some other drug. What is more, Southland Beach attracts substantial numbers of transients and people with criminal records, most of whom remain on the fringes of the beach, where they add to the potential for trouble.

Besides this diversity there is much uncertainty on the beach. It is not only that Southland Beach now attracts many tourists and inner-city people who know little about the beach or the ways of "beach people"; it is also apparent that even many regular beachgoers are uncertain about "what the regulations are" at Southland Beach. Even the clearly posted municipal ordinances regarding beach behavior are unknown to most beachgoers. What is more, beachgoers are typically unable to say what they would or should do if trouble were to occur. As Gibbs (1966) has observed, social rules (or "norms" in his usage) are often accompanied by "reactive" rules that indicate what should be done in reaction to a rule violation, and by whom. Knowledge of reactive rules at the beach, if indeed such beach rules can be said to exist at all, is uncertain, and this uncertainty could also increase the likelihood of trouble. For example, the majority of all beachgoers we spoke to were uncertain of the role and authority of lifeguards. All knew that they rescued people and most knew that they gave first aid, but only a small minority understood that lifeguards could or should be appealed to if trouble were to arise on the beach. Fewer still knew that each lifeguard tower had a direct telephone link to the police.

There is also uncertainty concerning the role of the police in reacting to beach trouble. A substantial minority of beachgoers thought that the police should not be on the beach at all, and most beachgoers had no idea how to obtain police assistance should they need it. Furthermore, very few beachgoers were found who felt that it was the responsibility of beachgoers themselves to take action should someone else be seen to be in trouble. Instead, what we found was a rampant individualism, or even isolation: each individual, or each member of a larger beachgoing group, seemed to feel that trouble should be ignored whenever possible, and if it could not be ignored, then it should be moved away from. In practice, as we often observed, this meant that trouble typically went unreported and unchecked, leaving the individual victim with no option but *sauve qui peut*.

This set of circumstances seems calculated to make Southland Beach a decidedly troublesome place during the crowded summer season, and yet people who go to this beach return to it again and again. Moreover, they say that they enjoy their beachgoing immensely and feel perfectly safe there. How can this be?

We shall begin our search for an answer by describing Southland Beach and the typical activities of people who go there. We shall examine the viewpoints and the activities of lifeguards and police officers who work there. We shall also report what various beachgoers say about the beach, and we shall consider what one is able to observe by systematically watching beachgoers' behavior. Special attention will be given to the vulnerability of women who come to the beach alone. In the final chapter we shall attempt to specify what allows beachgoers to get along with one another.

# 2

## Southland Beach

"Southland City" is a municipality of some 90,000 people in Southern California, and a part of the urban sprawl of Los Angeles. Its entire three-mile-long ocean frontage is a public beach, and has been since the city was founded before the turn of the century. Earlier in the century the beach was a famous resort; photographs from 1921, for example, show it completely packed with beachgoers wearing the bathing costume of that time and sitting under large umbrellas. It has remained popular and crowded ever since. The northern portion of Southland Beach is surrounded by one of the most expensive residential areas in Southern California. Adjoining the beach itself are private residences and beach clubs, which are still very fashionable and were once favored by many in the Hollywood movie colony when this area was known as "Rolls Royce Row." These large residences and clubs are separated by small parking lots, occasional refreshment stands, and public bathrooms. The yards of the large houses that adjoin the sandy beach often contain swimming pools, and they are set off from the public beach by fences of various kinds. There are only a handful of smaller, less expensive residences along this part of Southland Beach, which we shall call "North beach."

The southern half of the beach is bounded by small businesses and relatively inexpensive, sometimes run-down apartments. In contrast to North beach, "South beach" is flanked by a middle- to low-income community, parts of which some people refer to as a slum. Separating North beach from South beach is a municipal pier containing restaurants, amusement attractions (a merry-go-round, bumper cars, carnival games, and the like), and fishing facilities, including the right to fish from the pier without a license.[1] A six-lane highway parallels the beach along its northern portion, and smaller streets parallel the southern part. There are thirteen large city-run parking lots able to accommodate 5367 cars; the majority of these lots are along South beach or the area of North beach close to the pier. There are also numerous refreshment stands, 17 volleyball courts, and 11 large public bathrooms, one of which is mysteriously equipped with bidets.

According to City and County records for the last decade, in an average year some 12 million people visit this beach, with a high of almost 16 million being recorded in 1970. Over 50 percent of them come during the heat of the summer, in July and August, and another 20 percent do so in June and September. On a hot summer day, as many as 400,000 people are estimated to have crowded into this strip of sand, and weekend crowds of 300,000 in the summer are fairly common. It is this crowded, daytime summer beach activity that we shall attempt to describe. In doing so we must first recognize that while there are some clearcut patterns of beach behavior to be seen, there is also variation. People and their behavior vary from one part of the beach to another, and from one time of day to another. To provide an introduction to this complex and changeable urban beach setting, it will be necessary to describe some typical beach behaviors as well as those variations that depend on time, place, and the kind of people involved.

## Along Southland Beach

All of Southland Beach is clear white sand. There are no rocky areas, either on the sand or along the waterline. There

are lifeguard towers at 300-yard intervals all along the
beachfront. Unlike many beaches in Southern California,
however, Southland Beach is a remarkably variegated place,
with many of its various locales regularly attracting distinctive crowds of people who engage in beach activities that
differ somewhat from those seen in other areas. Beginning at
the southern boundary of the beach, there is a large area
(lifeguard towers 23-27) that attracts primarily younger
"Anglo" beachgoers.* (See accompanying figure.) Despite the
fact that this stretch of beach is paralleled by an unusually
large parking lot, this area is said by lifeguards to attract a
high percentage of local residents, including many young
families who live only a few blocks away. This observation

---

*"Anglo" is a local term used by many persons to distinguish white,
English-speaking Americans primarily from "Chicanos" (Americans
of Mexican descent) who are also white and may speak perfect English. Unlike "Paddy," a term Chicanos sometimes substitute for
Anglo, this term has few negative connotations in local usage.

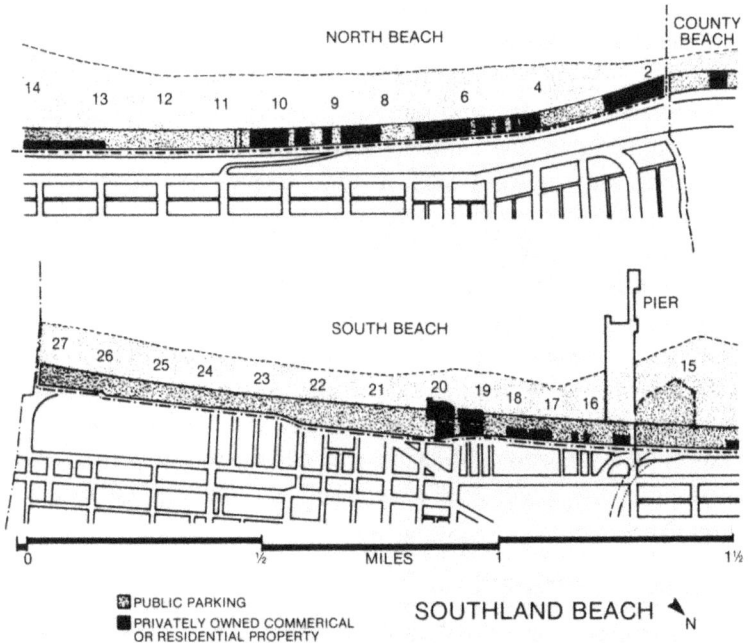

SOUTHLAND BEACH ↖N

appears to be correct, since some beachgoers in this area nod or say hello to one another, a practice that is rare elsewhere on Southland Beach. Even on crowded days this large parking lot remains half empty. Just north of this is an area of comparable size (lifeguard towers 18-22) which attracts primarily high-school-age surfers and their companions. A few years ago this area was considered one of the best surfing spots in Southern California. Today this area is reserved (at least much of the time) for "surfing only" with no swimming permitted. In most areas just the opposite is true except for early morning, late afternoon, and winter days when there are few swimmers to get in the way of and be endangered by surfboards. Like the more southern area, this area is almost exclusively Anglo, although here they are not primarily local residents.

To the immediate north is a smaller area (between towers 17 and 18) which seems to attract young families and young couples from all ethnic groups and primarily from non-local areas. From the northern edge of this area to the south side of the pier (towers 16 and 17) is the most diverse yet distinctive area along the entire beach. This area was formerly a showcase for weightlifters and gymnasts and some of this atmosphere remains, with a fenced grassy area often used by gymnasts of all ages, and with formal gymnastic competition or exhibitions sometimes taking place on the sand. This area is also unique because of the presence of a large array of gymnastic equipment—rings, parallel bars, jungle gyms—set back on the sand away from the water. There is also a place with playground equipment and toys for children, the only area of this kind on the beach. The area around tower 16 attracts a highly diverse population, including a high percentage of Chicanos and many non-English-speaking tourists. Indeed, all ethnic groups and all ages are represented, with young and old, Anglo and non-Anglo being about equally present. Many are tourists; some speak no English. With the exception of surfers, everyone and everything that can be seen along the entire beachfront can be seen here in a relatively small, often crowded area just south of the pier.

Beachgoers near area 16.

From just north of the pier to the south, the entire beach is paralleled by a paved walk and bikeway known as "the promenade."[2] From tower 18 to the south this promenade runs between the sandy beach itself and the parking areas. North of lifeguard tower 18 the walkway separates the sand from various structures, including a large and expensive apartment hotel, smaller and more rundown apartments, refreshment stands, and the like. In the area just south of the pier, there are some delapidated apartments,[3] long tables where old men play chess, the sandy patch equipped with children's toys, the grassy gymnastic area, several volleyball courts, half a dozen refreshment stands which sell beer among other things, a "head" shop, a shop that sells beach gear, and a large modern structure that is the lifeguards' headquarters.

The promenade is often crowded along its entire length, but at the area just south of the pier it becomes a true "promenade" with hundreds of persons, many of them dressed in street clothes, strolling back and forth, sometimes stopping to watch a volleyball game, to eat, or to rest. Some ride bicycles, weaving in and out of the strollers. Many of these strollers live or work in the area, but others come from far away, including tourists from foreign countries. The area is undeniably picturesque, and it attracts an extraordinary mixture of people, including teenage groups from the inner city, "jetsetters" from Beverly Hills, and local transients whose appearance is frequently both disheveled and bizarre. Some play musical instruments and one man sings operatic arias, usually without favorable comment from onlookers. While many of these people never venture onto the sand, this part of the sandy beach attracts the most diverse population seen anywhere along Southland Beach. The pier itself attracts many of these same people, who go there to eat, to play at carnival games of chance, or merely to stroll. Like the promenade, the pier, with its carnival atmosphere, attracts many people who never set foot on the sandy beach itself.

Passing under the pier to the north, there is another distinctive area, but one that is somewhat less crowded and diverse. This area, from the pier north to lifeguard tower 15, is unique because it is sheltered by a breakwater, providing a calm lagoon-like sea with only very small surf. This area is separated by buoys; one-half of it is reserved for swimmers and the other half for beginning surfers, and many inexperienced young surfers from all over Los Angeles come here. At the same time, presumably because of the supposedly safe water and ample parking, this area attracts large numbers of Chicano families from the inner city, none of whom surf, but instead wade and swim in the deceptively languid water. In fact, unpredictable currents can make this area treacherous for swimmers, and it gives lifeguards many headaches.

The next area to the north, due to the absence of nearby parking lots, is usually devoid of people, even on warm sunny weekends. It is known by lifeguards as "the desert." Another 300 yards to the north, however, there is a large parking lot, just at the place where the freeway exits onto the beach. This area around lifeguard tower 12 is heavily

Beachgoers near area 15.

crowded by people from the center of Los Angeles, the majority of whom are blacks or Chicanos. This lifeguard tower is
painted with Chicano "placas"—in this case, baroquely let-
tered names of East Los Angeles street gangs. While local
"beach people" never choose this part of the beach, many
Anglos from inland areas of Los Angeles do come here, pro-
ducing a highly heterogeneous population.

Two or three hundred yards to the north, however, is an
area that attracts primarily families of all ethnic groups, with
Anglos in the majority; and 300 yards north of this family
beach is another distinctive area (towers 8 and 9) that attracts
primarily young Anglos, most of whom swim or surf. The
area around one of these lifeguard towers attracts people
primarily from the local area, while the other attracts people
principally from the San Fernando Valley. "Valleys go home"
is painted on the first of these lifeguard towers, a reminder
that relations between young beachgoers in this area are not
always good. North of this is a large area (towers 2, 4, 6),
stretching to the northern limits of Southland Beach, that
attracts primarily family groups. Many of these people are
from the San Fernando Valley, although one small area is
almost exclusively used by people from Beverly Hills. No part
of Southland Beach, north or south, is segregated de facto by
age or ethnicity. It is possible to see an elderly couple in the
"surfers only" South beach area, and blacks, Chicanos, and
Asians sometimes settle down anywhere on the beach. But
certain parts of the beach do consistently attract certain kinds
of people.

There is nothing on the beach to mark the place where
Southland City ends and the jurisdiction of another city begins, and few if any beachgoers are aware that a change has
taken place. The sand is the same and so are the lifeguard
towers. The change is noticeable only by watching the Southland City police patrol unit turn and go back as it reaches the
northern or southern boundary of Southland City. Even
though this study will be focused primarily on the beach
within the limits of Southland City, the beach just north of its
invisible city line should not be ignored. This is so because it

contains unusual kinds of beachgoers, some of whom venture south along the sand into Southland Beach, and also
because these different kinds of beachgoers provide an instructive contrast with the people on Southland Beach.

This northern beach, which we shall call "County Beach,"
is one of the best known stretches of sand in Southern
California. It attracts preeminently local and regular beachgoers—"beach people"—and has done so for at least thirty
years. These beach people are typically upper-middle class
Anglos, and while some merely sun themselves or swim or
talk, as most people on the beach do, here people tend to
know each other and form groups that regularly meet on the
beach during the summer. Some of these groups persist for
many years. In addition to the couples, individuals, and
mothers with children who are common along the entire
beach, this area is known for its surfers, who are old as well
as young, and its volleyball players, which include professional and collegiate performers, as well as juniors and elders
of lesser skills. In part because of its volleyball stars and in
part because of its reputation as an "in" place, County Beach
also attracts various show business personages, many of
them lovely young women who wear the smallest but most
expensive bikinis available. In addition to these kinds of
beachgoers, County Beach has long been known for its "gay"
beach area. For many years gay men have assembled here in
an area one hundred yards or so north of the Southland
Beach line. On a warm and sunny weekend or holiday as
many as 1000 gay men crowd together on a small patch of
sand. Conditions sometimes become so crowded that some of
these men move north, where they may conflict with surfers,
or south into Southland Beach. In County Beach "the gays"
maintain a clear separation from non-gays. In other areas, no
such separation exists. The presence of gay men on County
Beach does not go unnoticed, as there are graffiti on nearby
walls saying such things as "fags go home," and one may
encounter a homemade sign stuck in the sand reading: "Fag
Beach, One Way" with an arrow pointing away from Southland Beach.

## Typical Behavior on Southland Beach

In summer, it is light by 6 A.M., with the sun making pastel colors on the sand and water. Later in the morning the seasonal overcast will usually block the sun, which does not shine through again until midday. On some summer days, especially in June, the sun never burns through the overcast. At 6 A.M. large vehicles are sifting, raking, and clearing the sand, a job they began in the dead of night. Partly because of these formidable trucks, one of which once decapitated someone sleeping on the beach at night, it is now illegal to sleep on the beach between midnight and 5 A.M. At this early hour there are other men on the beach, 15 in all, who rake up trash that the trucks miss. There are also a few men, mostly 50 or 60 years of age, who move slowly up and down the sand in the wake of the cleaning trucks using portable metal detectors in search of lost coins or other metal valuables. They keep their distance from one another and rarely lift their heads from the sand where their earphones tell them of a likely find. There is also an occasional yellow lifeguard vehicle preparing for the day, as well as a white police patrol car that periodically cruises the waterline.

Most of the people on the beach in the early morning are joggers, surfers, or fishermen. The joggers, most of whom are men, run on the wet sand near the water, their various costumes ranging from brightly colored (and expensive) running suits to ragged bathing trunks and T-shirts. Most are intent upon their exercise. They rarely speak, although one may nod or say hello to another as they pass. Women joggers run with particular single-mindedness. Because they see men at the beach at this early hour as being potentially dangerous, they say that they maintain a business-like manner in the hope of evading unwanted male attention. Even so, an occasional male jogger will run alongside a woman making comments that reveal his interest in seduction. One runs with a parrot on his shoulder, apparently as a conversation piece. As the women joggers go by, various fishermen who line the shore sometimes shout obscenities, and once in a while a

Surfers and girlfriend.

fisherman may enthusiastically expose himself. Most fishermen merely fish, however, while their families, who sometimes accompany them, sit forlornly in the cool damp morning, drinking coffee or reading.

At earliest light, surfers in their black wet suits are perched
atop their boards in the glassy, pewter-colored water. More
arrive during the breakfast hours, attempting to get in a few
good rides before school or work; others try to surf until the
crowds arrive and surfing becomes prohibited, as it is in midday between May 1 and September 30.[4] In these early hours
of the day, there is also an occasional individual doing calis-
thenics, or practicing kung fu or karate. There may also be a
shell gatherer or two, although this beach is not noted for tide
pools or shells. Now and then a fully dressed man walks
along with a camera, and other people in street clothes sit or
stroll—whether they are early risers or late retirees one cannot easily tell. There are also some ragged, disheveled men

who are apparently trying to shake off a long drunk and may have slept on the beach overnight despite the law. Religious devotees may also appear at dawn. For example, groups of nuns occasionally walk the sand, and persons in secular dress may sometimes be seen kneeling together in prayer, or sitting with hands upraised to the sky.

This scene changes as the joggers and surfers leave for breakfast and work, while others like them continue to arrive. By 8 or 10 A.M., depending on the day of the week and weather, the influx of daytime beachgoers begins. Although a few lifeguard towers open as early as 7, before 8 it is rare to see more than 100 or so people on the beach. By 10 on a cool weekday, 500 or 1000 people may have arrived; on a warm Saturday, Sunday, or holiday, many thousands may be on the beach by this hour.

## Mid-Day

While it is true that there are more young people than old people at this beach, and more white people than non-whites, there are many older people, just as there are many blacks, Chicanos, and Asians. There are also more women than men. In most areas of Southland Beach, about 60 percent of the teenaged or adult beachgoers will be female. Anywhere from 10 to 30 percent of all the people who come to the beach with someone will be women without male escorts. Perhaps 5 percent of all beachgoers are lone women. Young men without women also come to the beach in large numbers. In some areas of the beach fully half the beachgoers are over 30 years of age, and in several areas (particularly towers 12, 15, and 16) it is common for 30 to 40 percent of the beachgoers to be Chicano or black, and sometimes the percentage is larger than this.

Although there are some areas of the beach, as we have seen, that attract large numbers of local Southland City residents, along most of the beachfront local residents are a distinct minority. Various County and City surveys in recent years have estimated that approximately 85 percent of all beachgoers live many miles inland, with growing numbers of these coming from black or Chicano neighborhoods in the so-called "inner city."

Our own surveys confirm this pattern, showing that about 90 percent of all beachgoers are non-local residents. In one survey, 35 people of all ethnic groups were interviewed willy-nilly all along the beach; only 4 of these were from Southland City, with this number being matched by tourists from other states or countries; the remainder were from areas that are an average of 19 miles distant. In another survey, this time of 66 women of all ages, only 6 were from Southland City, four were tourists, and the remaining 58 traveled an average of 20 miles to the beach, one way. These figures might vary somewhat if larger samples were taken on some probability basis, but there can be little doubt that most people who come to this beach, including those who visit it several times a week, do so from considerable distances. There are two important consequences of this fact. First, people from all over Los Angeles County congregate at this beach; second, in order to do so, most of these people have traveled far, and have paid to park. We can suppose that they enjoy this beach greatly, or they would not go to so much effort to visit it.

Most beachgoers park in large city lots that charge $1.00 a day ($1.25 on weekends), although a few park in nearby metered spaces that charge 50¢ for five hours. Some park on unmetered streets as much as a mile away and walk to the beach. A few arrive by bus or live nearby and walk to the beach. Some beachgoers bring with them towels and blankets, food and drink (often including beer), radios, large styrofoam coolers, backrests, umbrellas, cameras, books and magazines, swim fins and rubber rafts, playing cards, backgammon sets, shovels, frisbees and balls of all sorts, as well as surfboards, dogs, barbeques, and many other things. Families who drive to the beach from the inner city usually make a day of it, and bring with them a great variety of beach gear. Local beachgoers, on the other hand, bring the absolute minimum: a large beachtowel, some suntan lotion, and perhaps a book, radio, or backrest.

Young women alone, in groups, and with boyfriends, arrive in their tight jeans or shorts and tanktops or T-shirts. They spread their towels out and wiggle out of their clothes attempting not to pull off their bikini bottoms as they do so. Most wear bikinis, but "string" or "knit" bikinis are not common, except at County Beach. After applications of suntan lotion, they lie on one side, then the other, often carefully undoing the straps of their bikini tops as they lie on their stomachs (nudity on this beach is illegal). They listen to their radios, read, chat, and sleep. Many fall asleep as soon as they arrive on the beach. Some sleep almost all the time they are there. From time to time they go to the water to wade or swim, or to a nearby refreshment stand, then return for more sun. Older women in their fifties and sixties also come to the beach alone or with friends. Such women usually, but not always, dress more modestly than younger women, and they receive less attention from men, but otherwise their routine is similar. Most of these women are deeply tanned. Being tan is highly desired by many women in Southern California, and a large number of women come to the beach with that goal in mind. Some men admit that they do the same.

Women of all ages bring small children to the beach. Sometimes several women band together, bringing all their youngsters with them. Such women usually place their towels on the berm, the sandy rise that separates the dry flat beach from the wet sand that slopes down to the water. Here they talk and sun themselves as they try to keep an eye on the kids, who build sand castles or wade in the shallow water. Other women may choose to lie anywhere on the sand and some select isolated areas 100 yards back from the water, but women with children are usually close to the water so that their children can play in the water and wet sand. This is less true around tower 16, where there is a playground for children far back on the sand next to the walkway. Such women must also cope with the needs of their children for food, drink, and bathrooms, so they usually choose areas which have such conveniences. For some of these women, their day at the beach seems to be anything but relaxing; others seem to be unruffled by their young charges and say that the beach is the easiest place they can think of to cope with children.

Younger men, especially teenagers, often come to the beach together. They frequently wear cutoff shorts rather than swimming trunks. After they settle down on the sand, they may play catch with a football or a frisbee. Many consume several cans of beer in an afternoon. Some sleep. Others swim. Most look and act bored. Surfers have little to do with non-surfers. They attend to the water and their boards and usually avoid interacting with people, except for the young women who often accompany them. Men in their twenties and thirties and older often come alone. Most lie on towels and set up backrests. Many prefer the berm, presumably because it is best for girl-watching, but others read or sleep, oblivious to everything around them. Many of these men go into the water to wade or swim briefly, but few swim far or body surf, activities which are dominated by younger people. Some men, particularly older ones, remain fully dressed, sometimes sitting in the sand, sometimes strolling up and down the beach. Some carry cameras, some obviously ogle women, and some merely watch the water or sleep. A few are panhandlers or drunks.

Couples of all ages come to the beach, usually to lie together without much conversation, enjoying the sun, the air, and the water. Many younger couples occasionally kiss and pet in a mild sort of way, but a few become passionate and uninhibited, apparently oblivious to the stares, furtive glances, or embarrassed avoidance they sometimes elicit from others. Necking of this sort occasionally occurs among older couples, including blacks and Chicanos, but it is primarily seen among teenaged Anglo couples.

Families and groups of friends are also common. Such groups, complete with their food and recreational equipment, can create an imposing spectacle as they tramp from parking lot to waterline, often as many as 12 or 15 strong. Such large groupings are especially common among Chicanos, who frequently include several generations in their beach parties. It is common for Chicanos and Chicanas alike to remain fully clothed on the beach. Even younger persons often do not wear bathing suits. Fully dressed or not, Chicanos frequently plunge into the water where they frolic or swim. They also engage in rough horseplay along the water's edge. The women typically sit and talk, usually in Spanish; many of these beachgoers speak little English. Blacks also come to the beach in large family groups, but they usually wear bathing suits. Unlike Chicanos, many blacks also come to the beach in couples or alone, and when they arrive they often act like any Anglo beachgoer, including tanning themselves in the sun.

All along the beach, then, people seem to find pleasure in what they do. They sun themselves, sleep, read, listen to radios, and play cards. Many swim, body surf, or wade; others stroll or run along the waterline. Many men glance at women; a few women glance back. Some men approach women; some women welcome their approach. Younger men play football, sometimes organizing games and playing tackle; men and women alike play catch with frisbees. Other men play soccer in the shallow water, or do exercises. A woman may look for a child she has temporarily lost sight of. Men and women play spirited games of volleyball, then shower off the sand, and swim. People stop to eat, opening their picnic lunches or buying pizza, corndogs, beer, or lemonade at a nearby refreshment stand. Many drink beer on the sand; some smoke marijuana. Here and there someone feeds seagulls, or takes photographs, or digs for sand crabs. Children dash happily to and fro. The sun is warm, the breezes are cool. The water is appealing. The sound of the surf is relaxing. There is a sensuous aura, too, created by so many beautiful near-naked bodies and the sense of escape from the problems of everyday life.

All of these enjoyable activities and sensations are a part of every summer day for large numbers of beachgoers, yet it would be wrong to give the impression that these people mingle with one another. With rare exceptions, people at the beach restrict their interaction to the person or persons with whom they came. They have only infrequent and fleeting encounters with "strangers." People may nod to one another, especially if they are walking along the waterline, they may ask a stranger for a match or the time, and they will toss back frisbees or balls that have gone astray. Interaction beyond these sorts of fleeting and impersonal exchanges is confined to small children, teenagers, surfers, volleyball players, and men who try to pick up women. All of these may at one time or another engage strangers in conversation or in play. The overwhelming majority of beachgoers—whether alone, in couples, or in larger groupings—almost always keep strictly to themselves. As much as anything else, this sense of isolation typifies Southland Beach.

Beachgoers begin to leave in some numbers about 2 P.M., and on an average day the majority have left by 3 P.M. But if the day is warm and the late afternoon fog does not roll in, quite a few people will stay until sunset, when the last lifeguard tower is closed for the day. Indeed, some people, particularly inner-city people, regularly arrive at the beach around 3 P.M. A handful of couples and families may stay on after sunset, sometimes barbequing dinner in a nearby parking lot. Some surfers continue to look for good rides, a couple of older men with metal detectors comb the sand, and joggers appear for their after-work exercise. A few lovers seek romance and solitude.

By nightfall, even on the warmest of nights, almost no one remains. Neither fires nor camping are permitted and sleeping on the beach after dark is discouraged by the police. A couple may park their car and walk across the sand to look at the moon glistening off the water, to stroll briefly, or to smoke marijuana, and a lone man may sleep, or walk along on an unknown quest. But at night, it is unusual for people to be on the beach. Only on the pier, where restaurants and arcades remain open until 12 P.M. or so, are there more than a few people after nightfall. Whoever the beachgoer may be, an average day at the beach is fun. But it is not always fun; there *can* be trouble.

### Trouble on Southland Beach

As one approaches the sand, many prominently located signs list the following ordinances: *"Municipal Code:* No fires or fireworks; no dogs permitted at any time; ball playing in

Beach ordinances and
grafitti.

designated areas only; must obey lifeguards' directions; no
dressing or undressing; no tents or enclosures permitted; no
sleeping midnight to 5 A.M.; must place rubbish in trash can;
no alcoholic beverages; no percussion instruments. *Penal
Code:* No disorderly conduct; no drunkenness or intoxication." As beachgoers cross the sand they are also likely to see
this sign, painted in the shape of a whale on the back of each
lifeguard tower: "Sorry folks, no dogs, horses, fires, or alcohol." As we shall see, many beachgoers plead ignorance of
these ordinances; others simply disregard them.

While Southland Beach is a place of great enjoyment for
many people, it is not without its hazards. There are three
common kinds of trouble at this beach. First, there is trouble
related to the water; second, there is trouble among ordinary
beachgoers themselves; third, there is trouble that results

from the activities of non-beachgoers who victimize persons on the sandy beach.

Water trouble is common, and it can be serious. Although sharks are present in these waters, at least at the present writing they have not consumed any swimmers along Southland Beach. Since the movie "Jaws," however, beachgoers often talk about sharks, rather nervously. Other fish such as barracuda do sometimes bite a swimmer, and both jellyfish and stingray are commonplace and inflict painful stings. In the summer of 1976 a seal bit a young woman swimmer and then tossed her in the air. Such attacks, fortunately, are rare. People also drown or come near to doing so. It is easy for a swimmer to overestimate his or her ability, and on days when the surf is high or riptides are present, the water can be extremely dangerous. People can also be in danger while body surfing if they misjudge a wave or are thrown into one another by the surf's force. They can be seriously injured if hit by a surfboard. And poor swimmers or non-swimmers can step into hidden holes and go in over their heads. People can also step on unseen glass, metal, or rocks in the shallow water, and older people or children who are wading in shallow water can be injured by an errant football or by the roughhouse play of young men.

Many beachgoers complain that the water is cold (even in the summer the daytime water temperatures are only in the upper sixties), or polluted (it is called "garbage surf" by some, but it is in fact safe for swimming, if not for all marine life). But the cold and the pollution are mere annoyances. Real water dangers are serious enough to call for the year-round presence of a sizable force of skilled and experienced lifeguards. In the course of a single day when the surf is high or riptides are particularly treacherous, these lifeguards may rescue scores of swimmers. In an average summer month— July 1975, for example—lifeguards on Southland Beach made 300 rescues, without any drownings. This is a remarkable record in view of the fact that an estimated 3,824,000 people went to the beach in that month, and that many of them almost certainly took foolish risks.

Trouble among beachgoers themselves is less well pub-

licized, but it is nevertheless noteworthy. Among the more
minor beach annoyances the following are common: loud
radios, sunburn, bee stings, stepping on glass, flip-tops, or
other litter, children kicking sand in the face of someone who
is lying down attempting to sleep or sunbathe, and dogs who
bark or bite or defecate on the sand where someone may sit.

Some equally common occurrences can be more annoying.
People sometimes place their towels or blankets too close to
another party, a practice that causes most people discomfort.
Men of all ages and descriptions stroll the beach, talking to
and often trying to pick up women. In many cases, this attention is unwanted and decidedly unpleasant. Teenagers, especially, may shout to or at one another in loudly obscene
fashion, frightening or appalling older people or families with
their children. Others, teenagers and older people alike,
drink beer or sometimes vodka, or smoke marijuana, and a
few become intoxicated, sometimes irritating or frightening
those around them. Some take other narcotics, especially
Quaalude.[5] A major source of annoyance is the common
practice by young men (and sometimes young women as
well) of playing catch with footballs or frisbees. People who
are lying on the sand, sometimes even sleeping, can be struck
by such a missile or trampled by someone who is running to
make a difficult catch.

Any of these problems can be moderately troublesome, but
there are others that can be of a still more serious and disturbing nature. For example, there are arguments on the beach
that sometimes lead to conflict. Some of these conflicts have
an interethnic or interracial dimension. Fights, including
brawls involving numbers of people, also occur. So does
theft, with the result that someone who leaves his or her
things to go for a swim or to buy refreshments may return to
find that a radio, wallet, book, towel, or everything has been
taken. Cars in parking lots are also broken into. Less common, but quite serious, are severe burns suffered by children
who fall into the coals of a beach barbeque. For this reason,
barbeques are prohibited, although some nevertheless appear
on the beach and are lighted. Other beachgoers allow their
children to dig deep holes in the sand. Sometimes such a hole

collapses, trapping and even suffocating a child before the sand can be dug away. Holes, like fires, are illegal, but they, too, continue to appear. People also lose their children with considerable regularity, and many hours of anguish may pass before the frightened child is located. For example, in July 1975, 200 children were reported lost, with 39 being lost on a single weekend day when an estimated 400,000 people crowded the beach.

Occasionally a child is sexually molested, usually while in the shallow water, a bathroom, or under the pier. And a regular feature of the beach landscape is provided by men who expose themselves. Known as "weinie waggers," these men provide a continuing source of amusement to some, and affront to others. Some expose themselves discreetly, but a few are astonishingly bold, walking about totally nude, or masturbating openly. The indecent exposure of men can offend beachgoers, and such activities sometimes lead to arrest. We are not aware that very many beachgoers have had their days ruined by the sight of lovely young women in skimpy bikinis, the tops of which sometimes briefly go astray. But some people do complain about the sight of grossly fat people in bathing suits, and others, especially mothers who have brought their children to the beach, are seriously offended by the heated necking of a nearby couple or two gay men.

Other problems are created by people who do not come to the beach to enjoy its sun or its water or its relaxing ambience, but come instead to victimize beachgoers. Whether by design or by chance, these fully clothed visitors to the beach often create serious problems. Some of the theft, especially strong-arm theft and breaking into parked cars, is done by non-beachgoers. Some men who expose themselves are outsiders as well, although many are regular beachgoers who just happen to expose themselves from time to time. Other men come to the beach to molest children, or to make a homosexual contact, or to make sexual advances to women. Rape occurs at night, and in recent years at least, at least one rape-murder has taken place in broad daylight on the sand. Several rapes have occurred in bathrooms during the day. Other people come to the beach to steal or buy drugs.

In addition to the theft and sexual crimes of outsiders, there are crimes of violence, including murder. Authorities all too commonly find bodies in the morning. Sometimes these are suicides, sometimes they are victims of a drug overdose, and sometimes, as in the case of a seriously wounded man found stuffed into a trash can, they are the victims of an unknown assailant. Some of the most serious threats of violence have involved teenagers who have come to the beach in search of gang combat, or to terrorize beachgoers, or sometimes to attack "fags." In an effort to minimize gang violence, the pier has sometimes been closed by the police on various holidays, including Memorial Day and July Fourth. For example, on July 4, 1976, a riot involving teenage gangs caused the police to make eight arrests and to close the pier for 90 minutes. Later that evening, the police reported two knifings and one shooting on the pier.

A less traumatic but nevertheless common and troublesome aspect of the beach is the large number of strange or frightening persons it attracts. Transient men, still drunk from the night before, may attempt to panhandle along the waterline. Persons who are high on drugs may wander the beach behaving in bizarre or intimidating ways. Apparent psychotics may shout or disrobe or collapse in a heap; others have seizures, and derelicts of the most pathetic appearance may appear when least expected or wanted, sometimes flopping down on the sand near ordinary beachgoers. Others pick through garbage cans in a fashion sure to upset all but the most insensitive. A mentally retarded youth may stare too openly at a woman, leading her to move away in discomfort, or a strangely robed religionist may loudly exhort everyone to abandon all pleasures of the flesh, then tear off his clothes and run for the water.

All of these things can happen at Southland Beach. Yet apparently they do not happen often enough, or are not taken seriously enough, to spoil the pleasure of the millions of persons who go to this beach every year. The potential for trouble clearly exists, and trouble does occur, but apparently it does not get out of hand.

# 3

# The Lifeguards

The popular vision of a Southern California lifeguard, confirmed by so many novels and movies, is that of a tall, blond, deeply tanned, athletic young man watching carefully over the safety of swimmers while beautifully bronzed young women in their bikinis loll expectantly in the background. The vision is not entirely fiction. Many lifeguards are tall and blond. All swim superbly. All take water safety seriously. Their towers are ringed by beautiful young women, and romance can blossom. Even before World War II, this image was popularized by two Southern California beach lifeguards, Buster Crabbe and Johnny Weismuller.

As one might expect, however, the Hollywood stereotype of a lifeguard is not always accurate. Many lifeguards are not blond; indeed, some have dark hair and a few are balding. In fact, on Southland Beach, one lifeguard is Asian, another is Jewish, one (who is particularly respected by his peers) has a Spanish surname, and one—more wondrous still—is a woman. Not all are pursued by admiring beach beauties; the tastes of such women for heroic men are said by lifeguards to have changed toward hairier and hipper types. Many lifeguards in turn pay only passing attention to bikinied women on the beach. Some lifeguards are "beach people" who were almost raised on the sand and who remain in love with the surf and sun. Others were raised far from the beach and have no great love for the ocean. A few of these see lifeguarding as nothing more than a job, albeit one that pays well.

All lifeguards at Southland Beach are hired by the County of Los Angeles, Department of Beaches. They have a standard training, follow a manual of procedures, and wear a uniform—red boxer-style trunks, a white T-shirt, and a dark blue windbreaker—all marked with inconspicuous insignia. They are all outstanding swimmers, they have excellent vision, and they want to prevent drownings. Although some lifeguards were relatively unfamiliar with the ocean before becoming guards, all have been competitive swimmers, and all have passed a series of demanding tests of their ability to swim in the ocean. All this equips lifeguards admirably for their first responsibility—water safety. But lifeguards are also called upon to play an important role in maintaining social order on the beach, and for this role they are less well prepared.

### The Southland City Lifeguard Service

In 1975, the Southland City Lifeguard Service consisted of a Captain, seven full-time lifeguards of various ranks, and 80 "recurrent" or seasonal guards, who work on a regular basis during the summer months, but only as needed during the winter. Most of these guards—"tower guards"—work in one of 20 lifeguard towers that are distributed along the entire beachfront at intervals of approximately 300 yards. The towers are solid wooden compartments with windows and doors set up some six feet in the air on heavy wooden supports, and given access to the water by a sloping wooden ramp. The towers are set close to the high tide line and permit direct visual inspection of the surf in front and on either side. Some towers are regularly manned by more than one guard. Backing up the tower guards are four vehicles, including a dune buggy "call car," which can quickly drive across the sand with emergency paramedical equipment and trained personnel. A large, modern headquarters building is located just south of the pier. Each tower has a direct telephone linkage to a central switchboard at headquarters. This switchboard may relay any call to headquarters personnel or to the police.

Prior to 1932, there was no formal lifeguard service on Southland Beach. The first towers were simple platforms perched on top of 10 foot poles, with ladders for access. In these early days, lifeguards—who even then were outstanding swimmers with good lifesaving training—communicated with one another by means of signal flags. As early as 1935, however, there was an emergency vehicle that supported the guards in the towers. And, even then, lifeguards had to cope with problems that had nothing to do with water safety. For example, they had to make sure that men kept buttoned both of the shoulder straps on their one-piece suits. In those days men apparently thought it was stylish to affect a one-shoulder, Tarzan look, and this was not at all in keeping with prevailing notions of beach modesty.

At the present time, Los Angeles County lifeguards are probably the highest paid and perhaps the best trained lifeguards in the world. For example, a permanent beach-guard receives a starting salary of over $16,000 per year, and a Captain earns over $24,000. Rookie guards receive a starting wage of $5.44 an hour. All lifeguards must pass a 16-hour course in emergency medical treatment, as well as various swimming and physical tests. In one such test, upwards of 500 aspiring lifeguards rush pell-mell into the surf, swim to a buoy 250 or 300 yards out, turn right for one mile, then elbow and punch their way around a final buoy while returning to the shore. The first 80 finishers are eligible for hiring as recurrent guards. Permanent lifeguards must learn, in addition, more advanced paramedic skills (a 40-hour course), especially cardiopulmonary resuscitation and the treatment of spinal injuries. (Los Angeles County lifeguards are considered to be especially skillful in the treatment of spinal injuries.) They also must qualify in rescues involving lifeguard boats, scuba gear, and cliff climbing. These permanent guards also attend a 68-hour course at the Los Angeles County Sheriff's Department Academy for partial training in law enforcement, and each graduate is deputized as a law enforcement officer. Guards must also qualify in repeated refresher courses. Recurrent guards receive no formal training in law enforcement or in the management of non-water related beach problems. What they learn about these matters, they learn as they go along. As a large and successful part of County government, these men, and now women as well, are part of a closely supervised organization that has one overriding commitment —the prevention of drowning.

### Water Safety: The Primary Responsibility

For the Los Angeles County Lifeguards, nothing is as terrible as a drowning. Lifeguards on the "front lines," as they put it, watch the water continually, not only to rescue swimmers who appear to be in trouble, but also to prevent trouble in the water *before* it can occur by calling or helping endangered swimmers out of the water. Each guard on the beach carries at all times a bright orange, plastic rescue float; should a swimmer in trouble be seen, the guard and his rescue "can" are in the water without delay.

The success of this water safety approach is demonstrated by the extraordinary infrequency of drowning along County beaches. Along all Los Angeles County beaches from 1965 to 1975, there have been a reported 259 million beachgoers. Of these, 1,576 required cardiopulmonary resuscitation, but only nine persons drowned. In 1974, when a record estimate of 40 million people went to these beaches, there were 102 resuscitations, and only two drownings. In addition, 1,328 swimmers were called out of the water in order to prevent the danger of drowning. In July of 1975, on Southland Beach alone, there were 300 rescues, with as many as 30 occurring in a single day, and three times these numbers of preventions—that is, calling swimmers out of the water. Not one of the estimated 11 million visitors to Southland Beach in 1975 drowned. It could well be otherwise. For example, in 1973, San Diego had an estimated 7.4 million beachgoers, seven of

whom drowned; and on the island of Oahu, in Hawaii, where
the surf is admittedly larger than it is in Southern California,
35 of an estimated 2.8 million beachgoers drowned the same
year (*Ocean Lifeguard*, 1975). By any standard, the water safety
record of Los Angeles County lifeguards is impressive.

Lifeguards are trained to regard the ocean as totally
treacherous and to scan the water constantly for any sign that
a swimmer may be in trouble. They scan as they stand in their
towers, sometimes with binoculars to their eyes, and they
scan as they walk back and forth along the waterline. They
watch each swimmer who enters the water for an indication
of his or her ability—how the person enters the surf, how
well he or she swims, how far out the swimmer goes. They
frequently monitor each swimmer's progress as well, recalling how long the person has been in and looking for signs of
fatigue or distress. Often a mere glance is enough, but sometimes binoculars are used, or the guard goes off on foot to
have a closer look at someone who worries him. Lifeguards
agree that it takes three summers for a guard to become truly
skillful. Before that, signs can be missed, and errors of judg-
ment can be made. Fortunately, rookie guards are taught to
err on the side of caution by calling people out of the water
earlier than necessary, and they are flanked by more experienced lifeguards who can back them up when necessary.

The lifeguards' record of safety can only be appreciated
when the problems they face are understood. Bad weather is
one. On a summer day in 1975 the surf rose to 8 or 10 feet,
and after making innumerable rescues, all bathers were finally ordered out of the water. In past years, erratic spring
weather has led to such horrendous water problems that 300
or 500 rescues have had to be made in a single day; some
guards spent 12 consecutive hours making one rescue after
another. On such days, the riptides are huge and the bottom
is still pocked by holes ground out by winter storms. In general, however, most lifeguards believe that they are more
likely to prevent water trouble when riptides—the greatest
killer—are present. At such times, the guards are tremend-
ously alert and watchful. They say it is when the ocean is

lovely and calm, and they are correspondingly relaxed, that someone in trouble may go unnoticed.

Another problem is the administration of first aid for minor beach hurts. Beachgoers come to the towers with all manner of injuries, from the painful wounds inflicted by stingrays or jellyfish, to cut feet, to bee stings. Attending to all of these takes time and can deflect a guard's attention from the water. A bee sting, for example, can be particularly distracting, as when bees sting women under their bikini tops—a common occurrence, it seems. Such women, sincerely in pain, rush to the tower for help, and often unabashedly remove their tops to provide an uncluttered view of the sting. As one guard put it, "you have to find out if the stinger is still in, but it's embarrassing to be up there on a tower in front of everyone with a bare-boobed woman." If not embarrassing, it is at least distracting as are more mundane injuries. More serious is the continual problem posed by persons who enter the water while intoxicated, by alcohol or narcotics, and often suffer shock as a result. Guards watch closely for such people and try to head them off before they can get into the water.

Surfers pose another problem. Quite a few lifeguards used to be surfers, and some still are. These men are very sympathetic to the plight of surfers, who each summer day at 10 or 11 A.M. are chased out of the surf to leave it free and safe for swimmers. Surfboards are dangerous to swimmers, as everyone knows; but as surfers know, to be forced out of the water just as the surf is getting good is a painful disappointment. Surfers have been known to shout derision at lifeguards who try to get them out of the water, calling them "surf-pigs." On some occasions, lifeguards have been openly defied and have been forced to call the police to arrest surfers who refused to leave the water.

More troublesome still are the growing numbers of "inner-city" beachgoers, both black and Chicano, who lack even rudimentary knowledge of either the ocean or swimming. Lifeguards agree that such persons make them very nervous, not only because they are in danger but also because they may misinterpret a lifeguard's concern for their safety as an unwarranted show of "Anglo" authority. In general, lifeguards say that black beachgoers, most of whom are poor or inexperienced swimmers, are cautious and usually stay in shallow water and take few risks. They say that Chicanos, on the other hand, despite equally poor swimming abilities, plunge out into deep water, often fully clothed. These reckless swimmers often resent "interference" from lifeguards and confrontations can sometimes ensue.

Ironic as it may seem, many swimmers are embarrassed when a lifeguard swims out to "save" them, feeling that their ability as swimmers is being challenged. Such people may refuse to take the rescue float and may try to swim ashore by themselves. Experienced guards sometimes try to cope with such swimmers by letting them reach the point of exhaustion before offering them the "can" for a second time and dragging them ashore. The problem arises because swimmers typically overestimate their ability to swim ashore through heavy surf, a difficult task even for a fresh swimmer unless he is both skilled and experienced. Lifeguards understand a swimmer's pride, but when a lifeguard believes that someone is about to "eat it" (drown) he will usually "hit the water" right away. The swimmer's pride must be a secondary concern.

Whether by training or by temperament, lifeguards truly enjoy making rescues. They actually compete for the opportunity of saving someone, and they experience joy—as well as praise—when they succeed. An experienced lifeguard on Southland Beach will average 40 rescues a year. Even older guards now in a supervisory role at headquarters sometimes "get the fever" and want to make a rescue. As one such guard put it, "There's no feeling better than the realization that because of you a person is still alive. There was one time when I pulled in a teenaged girl and her grandfather. They were going down together and I pulled them both in. After that the girl came back to my tower every day to thank me. . . . Another time, several years ago, there was a seven-year-old girl who had drowned. She was the deepest purple I've ever seen in my life. We did mouth-to-mouth and heart massage, but she started going into convulsions. We rushed her to the hospital and kept up the resuscitation all the way. We had to leave her there. Two weeks later I'm working the tower and here she comes to thank us for saving her. Her father was with her and he was crying. Out of all the time of being a lifeguard that was the most fulfilling moment I've seen. I still break up when I think about that girl."

### Behind the Tower

Not everything lifeguards do is so fulfilling. Relatively little of their time is actually spent making rescues. Instead, some of their time and energy must be spent coping with problems that occur on the beach behind their towers. Consider the following story from an experienced lifeguard who recently transferred from a less urban beach to Southland Beach: "Let me tell you about my first day here. I was in tower 18 on the South beach; it was a cool morning, overcast. All of a sudden I saw this white guy running down the beach being chased by a cop who had his club out. Another cop hanging onto a harbor patrol vehicle was trying to head him off. As the cop catches the guy, the guy pulls a knife on him. His eyes were rolling like he was really drug crazed. The cop pulls up now and leaps out with his .38 drawn and points it at the kid's head and yells, "freeze." I mean here is a fully-loaded .38 that would have blown that kid away but he doesn't freeze, he keeps slashing at the cops with this knife and now the cops are both beating on him with their clubs. I'm on the phone calling for ambulances because I *know* somebody is going to get killed. Finally the kid breaks away and runs in the water with the cops right after him, spit-shined shoes, blue uniform, and all. They got him in a choke hold and I'll tell you, they made him remember them. That was my *first* day! Fortunately there are quiet, peaceful days here too!"

A ten-year lifeguard said: We've got this laid back, watch-the-girls image, but what we really face is a paramilitary problem." Not all guards would state the case that baldly. Indeed, some believe that Southland Beach is usually a quiet, family-oriented place. But all would agree that what goes on behind the tower *can* be a problem. In fact, tower lifeguards must cope with some kinds of beach problems every day. The most common are dogs, deep holes, and barbeques. Intoxicated persons who attempt to swim are also common, as are fully dressed people who may pose a menace to beachgoers. Lifeguards often watch such persons and sometimes they are approached by them. For example, a fully-dressed woman may approach a tower to declaim loudly about sin and resurrection. A man may behave strangely, as happened during the summer of 1976, when an otherwise unremarkable appearing person attempted to sell his daughter to a lifeguard; or someone may issue an incoherent complaint about something or other before wandering off. Some of these episodes can be amusing, but they all take the lifeguard's time and attention. There is nothing amusing about the responsibility of telling beachgoers to remove their dogs, fill in holes, put out barbeques, or stop drinking.

Lifeguards must also be alert to more serious problems such as theft, violence, and sexual molestation. Where these kinds of problems are concerned, lifeguards often become more actively and personally involved. When water conditions permit, many lifeguards watch closely for potential thieves, monitoring a suspicious person's progress across the sand. Sometimes they watch such a person because a beachgoer alerts them, but other times they do it on their own. On occasions, lifeguards have seen a theft actually taking place, as for example in the case of a shabbily dressed man who slid along the sand on his belly until he could reach the wallet of someone who was swimming at the time. In this instance, and others like it, the lifeguard will call for the police then go out on the sand and detain the suspect until the police arrive, usually asking for a lifeguard "call car" to back him up in case of resistance.

Violence is even more troublesome. Its most alarming form is perhaps ethnic gang fights. These have occurred on numerous occasions on Southland Beach, with gangs of marauding blacks attacking white beachgoers, or Chicano gangs fighting black ones, or most often, two Chicano groups fighting one another. These fights often involve weapons such as knives and chains, and typically they leave badly injured victims behind. As one guard put it: "You'll be watching the water, and when you look behind the tower there are about 50 Mexican kids right out of central casting—you know, chains and knives. One kid had the Last Supper tattooed on his back." In some fights lifeguards have defused the action by appealing to gang members' girlfriends to break it up before the police arrive; in others, they have huddled in their towers helplessly waiting and hoping for the police; and on a few occasions, they have actually dived into the water where they swam about safely until help arrived. "There can be real tension when you see a group of black guys all dressed for trouble. You say to yourself, 'Oh no,' and you don't know what to do. You're on the edge of your seat. If anything happens, you think, how fast can I get into the water?" These fights were so troublesome some years ago that each tower was supplied with an axe handle for defense, and guards today talk about using their hard plastic rescue cans as weapons should the need arise.

Lifeguards must also be concerned with family fights (one summer during this research a man beat his wife severely around tower 10), fights between women, and those involving gay men, who are sometimes victimized by "straights," particularly by groups of teenagers. In all these instances, guards believe that it is foolhardy to become involved personally: "People like that are ready to kill, I mean kill." Another said, "It's like walking into a fight between Muhammed Ali and Joe Frazier." In violent confrontations of this sort, guards try indirectly to minimize the conflict while they watch anxiously for the arrival of the police officers they have called for.

It is in the area of sexual offenses against women and children that lifeguards probably show the greatest concern and personal commitment. Lifeguards say that women should be able to come to the beach without being "hassled," yet they recognize that men seeking pick-ups are an everyday feature of the beach and that some men—known as "walkers"—do nothing but cruise the length of the beach trying to pick up women. Lifeguards sometimes see what they call "soft-core flashing"—a man wearing loose trunks sitting or lying with his legs wide apart so that his genitals are exposed in an apparently inadvertent manner. Such persons are usually left alone, because criminal conviction would be almost impossible. More open "flashers," or masturbators, or men who touch women, are likely to receive personal attention from a lifeguard who witnesses the act.

Lifeguards discuss among themselves the rapes or molestations of women that have occurred—or are said to have occurred—on the sand on a crowded day. One instance, in which a Hollywood starlet was raped and murdered on the sand three years earlier, particularly sticks in their minds. They discuss this crime among themselves and worry about other attempted rapes that have been reported on the sand. Perhaps as a result, this comment is characteristic of many guards: "I feel protective of women on the beach. If I see a guy move in on a woman and put his arm around her or something, I'll get over there and walk by real close to be sure she's OK." Another lifeguard said: "When I first started I used to be embarrassed. I asked guys like that politely to leave the beach. I didn't want to get them in trouble and I didn't want to cause a big scene at the beach. But after hearing of numerous rapes and a sexually related murder, I started either reporting them or arresting them right away."

Guards frequently take quick action in episodes like this. For example, in June of 1975, a lifeguard on South beach was watching the sand when he saw a "flasher" easing toward a pretty girl who was lying on the sand. Suddenly the man leaped on top of the girl. At this the lifeguard yelled to his partner in the tower to call the police and ran to the girl's aid, wrestling the man off her and holding him until the police arrived, while the girl screamed in shock and terror. Another guard has several times arrested men who have exposed themselves too openly or masturbated on the beach. "We had a walker this summer on North beach. This guy was masturbating at these girls. They've got it down to a science you know. Just whip it out of the trunks; maybe they have quick-release trunks like Frederick's of Hollywood. I saw the whole thing and went down and arrested the guy."

Most guards have liberal attitudes towards sex. They like to look at beautiful women, and they don't object when teen-agers "make out" on the sand, or even when men discreetly "hustle" women on the beach. They laugh uproariously about the occasions, which have happened, when male beachgoers have complained about girls exposing themselves by dropping their bikini tops. They tolerate men who bring cameras with right-angle lenses to the beach to get intimate photographs of unsuspecting women. But they draw a line at more overt sexual violations, and are often willing to take action, even before the police arrive.

A final beach problem is perhaps the most sensitive and troubling of all. Lifeguards who work in areas where there are large numbers of Chicano or black beachgoers admit that they are often tense and uncomfortable. It is not just the poor water knowledge of these people that bothers the lifeguards, it is their perceived unpredictability and readiness for con-frontation. Both Chicanos and blacks usually come to the beach in large family groups. Chicanos must often be told— in faltering Spanish—that their barbeque, or their raft, or their beer is illegal. Unfortunately, misunderstandings some-times occur. Black beachgoers strike some guards as being unnecessarily antagonistic. When either blacks or Chicanos come to the beach in groups of several males in street clothes, tension is inevitable. Guards watch such groups warily for signs of trouble. Some guards, especially those who speak adequate Spanish, say that "ethnic" beachgoers are no more trouble than ordinary Anglo beach people, but most guards believe that these "ethnics" do bring tension to the beach, in part because their beach behavior is unpredictable, particu-larly with regard to flare-ups of violence or drunkenness.

One guard recalled an afternoon when Chicano teenagers inexplicably threw stones at his tower. Another mentioned an occasion one summer day when 10 or 12 Chicanos set up their blankets and beach equipment right under his tower (it is common for Chicanos to do this in order to take advantage of the shade the tower provides), and began systematically to consume three cases of beer. The guard became increasingly nervous as their voices rose and quarrels seemed about to erupt into violence. To his amazement, boxing gloves were brought out and for the better part of an hour the Chicanos took turns punching one another. They had a marvelous time, but left behind a puzzled and nervous lifeguard. Many lifeguards feel that Chicanos and blacks resent and reject their authority. "I tell some family to do something for their own safety and I hear, 'goddam white honky' and I just get fed up. I'm only trying to keep them alive."

An experienced lifeguard had this view: "We've been taught that you've got to watch blacks and Mexican-Americans because of their poor swimming ability. So automatically when a group comes to the beach you just go, 'oh,' and a mental image goes into your brain to keep an eye on those people. It's also compounded when they are drinking, and they very often are. They also bring so much illegal equipment—18 innertubes, 72 plastic mats, and 47 lifejackets. Those things don't help you in the water, in fact they're dangerous. We don't even allow lifejackets because more people could drown easier with a damn lifejacket on than they can with it off. That's because a lot of times people will roll face down and they can't turn over. . . . Sometimes we don't understand them and they don't understand us, but you have to understand that the great majority of these people are just coming to the beach to have fun. For them, it's a big family outing. They work their butts off all week trying to make enough money to bring their family and their barbeque down here and really make a day of it. It's different, I mean they really make a grand appearance when they arrive carrying an entire surplus store with them, but it's all right." It's just a different cultural thing and we don't have to get uptight about it. When we tell these people not to do something they usually understand it's for their own good."

### Lifeguards and the Police Role

Lifeguards agree that if they enforced all the relevant beach ordinances they would have no time left to maintain water safety, and some guards dislike enforcing any ordinances, saying "I feel like I'm here to save lives, not play cop." The water clearly comes first, but all guards recognize that there are beach problems which must be dealt with. Most tower guards are delighted to pass on the responsibility for coping with most beach problems to their supervisors or the police. But when beachgoers are in trouble, they are far more likely to run to a lifeguard than they are to call the police. As the lifeguards say, they are indeed on "the front line." Over 90 percent of the people interviewed on the beach said that they would go to a lifeguard if they needed first aid. About one-third of these people would go to a lifeguard if "something really upset" them. About 20 percent said that they would report a theft to a lifeguard and about 15 percent said that they would do the same with regard to indecent exposure. Whether they like it or not, lifeguards have beach problems brought to them.

If a serious problem is brought to a lifeguard, he will usually call for the police. Sometimes the complaint is so confused or the person who makes the complaint is so unconvincing that a lifeguard may choose to investigate before making a call, or to do nothing at all. Where less serious problems are concerned, most lifeguards use considerable discretion. Thus, amost all guards overlook the inconspicuous use of alcohol or marijuana. A beer or two is simply not an issue, nor usually is a fair degree of intoxication unless, as we have seen, the drunk heads for the water or threatens another beachgoer. Then the guard will intervene. All guards also know that marijuana is common on the beach, but with rare exceptions they ignore its use as well. Dogs, which are strictly illegal at all times, receive highly varied attention. Some guards believe that dogs and the beach go together; others worry about dogs that chase children, bite them, or defecate on the sand and regularly tell beachgoers to remove their dogs. Only a few would actually call the police to come and arrest a dog owner, however, and that would be done in an extreme instance—such as a vicious dog threatening people or an owner refusing to obey several requests by the lifeguard.

Holes and fires, both of which are illegal and dangerous to children, receive similarly varied attention. Most guards make serious efforts to protect peoples' children from suffocation or burns, but a few sometimes look the other way. There is more consensus regarding "psychos," at least when they are known as regular beachgoers and as harmless. All guards know many such people, and although they may refer to them in jocular manner as "wind-up-man" or "crazy Helen," in reality they not only tolerate them but even protect them from the dangers posed by the ocean or uncaring beachgoers. In some cases, however, a person is perceived as being dangerous, or in danger, and lifeguards take action. For example, during the summer of 1975 a lifeguard arrived at his tower in the early morning to see a young man standing fully clothed in water above his waist while he drank a can of malt liquor. The man ignored the lifeguard's order to leave the water. Whether he was drunk or psychotic or both was immaterial. He was in danger and the police were called.

If the police are not called, the lifeguard must handle the problem by himself, and even if the police are called, the lifeguard must control the situation until the police arrive. He is often highly uncomfortable in this role. Lifeguards agree that they are almost completely untrained to deal with the "law and order" problems that the people on the sand create. Only the permanent guards have had any formal police training, and their training is not comparable to that given police officers. As lifeguards see it, police officers have not only the requisite training but also the "blue uniform" that symbolizes the traditional authority to cope with crime, on the sand or anywhere else. Lifeguards have no symbolic indication of their authority. As they put it, "Here we are in our red trunks trying to deal with criminals. We go out and try to handle a problem and you can just see people thinking, 'Who's this clown in the red suit?' They don't really know how to react to you."

The problem lifeguards face is exemplified by the experience of a permanent guard who saw a violent confrontation in a parking lot and rushed to break it up. When he arrived he found two men facing each other down—one armed with a crowbar and the other with a speargun. Dressed only in his red trunks, the guard talked them into putting their weapons down and backing away from one another. As he saw it, they were relieved that a third party gave them the excuse not to use their weapons. But when the lifeguard asked to see their identification they not only refused, but were derisive, saying "Who the hell are you?" A moment later a police officer arrived and immediately asked for identification. The two men quickly and deferentially complied.

Lifeguards also report incident after incident in which beachgoers have arrogantly refused to comply with their requests or even their direct orders. Nevertheless, a few lifeguards, particularly the permanent guards, are reasonably confident about their ability to handle beach problems. Some even run great risks. For example, in the summer of 1974, a young woman ran to lifeguard tower 8 to say that her friend was being raped in a nearby bathroom. The two lifeguards in the tower first called the police, then ran to the bathroom, dashing inside without knowing whether they would face knives, guns, or merely violent young men. Luckily, the two young men were unarmed and the lifeguards were able to hold them until the police arrived. Other guards have taken similar risks.

To compound the problems that lifeguards face in carrying out a police role, they are expected by the County to cope with problems in a "low-key" manner. This means that they are expected to avoid making arrests or issuing citations in order not to alienate themselves unnecessarily from the citizens whose lives they are there to protect. (A recurrent guard must make a citizen's arrest like anyone else, but permanent guards have police authority.) Under such restraint—without visible or recognized authority, unarmed, and feeling themselves untrained for police work—many lifeguards try to cope with beach problems by adopting a "good guy" role in which they offer friendly advice to a beachgoer: he should really get his dog off the beach, or stop drinking, or whatever, "because it's against the law, and the police will be patrolling any minute now, and no one wants to get a ticket, do they?"

As some guards see it, this allows them to maintain rapport with beachgoers while enforcing the law. Others recommend a "robot" strategy, saying that the best approach is simply to say that the law is thus-and-so, and lifeguards are ordered to enforce the law, and that, quite simply, is that. Who can argue with a robot, they ask? Nothing personal is involved.

Most lifeguards see the problems of coping with beach behavior as being more complex than this, agreeing that given their lack of effective training and well-recognized authority, what counts most is the personality of the guard. Thus, some guards regularly make trouble out of nothing by their hostile, insulting manner, while others have a genius for cooling off the most volatile situations. One senior guard is said to speak so slowly and calmly that by the time he has said "what's going on?" everyone has forgotten what they were arguing about. Another senior guard is notorious for getting into fistfights with beachgoers over matters that most lifeguards regard as trivial.

A final consideration has to do with the reluctance of many guards to take a police role at all. More experienced lifeguards may take such a role, and some do so eagerly. Less experienced guards usually dislike the role and avoid taking it as much as possible. There are many reasons, then, why lifeguards are not always effective or comfortable in dealing with beach problems, particularly serious ones. It should come as no surprise that lifeguards clearly recognize the need for police protection on Southland Beach. From their twenty towers up and down the beach, lifeguards can observe beach problems as they take shape, and they are available to receive complaints from offended beachgoers. Their telephones can bring the police to the scene quickly. These telephones are a kind of lifeline, because however much the lifeguards do to maintain social order on the beach, they need the police, and they know it.

In years past it took time for a police patrol car to arrive at the beach, and when it did the officers had difficulties walking or running across the sand in their standard blue uniforms and black leather shoes. Anywhere from five to

fifteen minutes could elapse between call and arrival, depending on the code priority given the problem, and most
often the suspect had vanished before the police officer arrived. As guards typically put it, "When people on the beach
start yelling and screaming, we need a cop *right now!*" In an
effort to provide better police patrol, faster response to trouble and more mobile police officers, a beach patrol vehicle—
Unit 99—came into being.

To a man, the lifeguards welcomed this new police re-
source, but when they were asked to ride with the police in
making routine beach patrols, almost 90 percent of the
lifeguards objected. Some did not want to acquire "a police
image," others insisted that the water was their interest, and
some no doubt had private reasons. Nevertheless, this beach
patrol vehicle went into service in the summer of 1974 and
some lifeguards did ride on patrol with police officers. The
reasons given for pairing a lifeguard with a police officer are
somewhat conflicting, but it appears that the police had a
shortage of available personnel and thus could not spare two
officers, and it was apparently thought by some officials that
having a lifeguard on this patrol would not only help with the
patrol but would also be good for public relations and
lifeguards could also administer first aid if needed.

The lifeguards who rode along on these 1974 patrols had
varied reactions. One guard, who was a physically powerful
man with a black belt in karate, thought it was an entirely
positive experience. He found the police to be reasonable
men and their patrols to be effective. Another guard hated
the experience. He thought that several officers, if not all,
were unnecessarily curt and sometimes even cruel. A third
lifeguard fell in between these extreme opinions. He found
two or three officers to be excellent, but thought another was
sometimes too abrasive. More importantly, this guard spoke
for all the lifeguards by saying that Unit 99 was an excellent
innovation that made the lifeguards' job much easier. Thus
although most guards still resist police patrol duty (such patrols by lifeguards were made only occasionally after 1974),
they agree that Unit 99 provides an effective visual deterrent

for certain kinds of beach problems (especially gang violence), that it can react rapidly to emerging trouble, and that it helps lifeguards in watching the water to know that the police are available when beach problems arise.

## Conclusion

Lifeguards talk about Southland Beach in conflicting ways. Some think of it as a mellow, family-oriented place where people can enjoy themselves and experience some beauty. These guards say that "the beach really runs itself." But others say that Southland Beach is "tense," "ugly," and "weird." One experienced guard said that it was a likely spot for the outbreak of World War III. Most give the impression that they are ambivalent about the beach as a whole. Lifeguards clearly love the water; it is *their* environment. Yet most lifeguards see the sandy part of the beach as becoming less and less pleasant. They speak of the diminishing numbers of "beach people" who truly love and respect it, and the increasing intrusion of the "city atmosphere." More exactly, they talk about Southland Beach as a melting pot at the end of a freeway, a playground for people from the inner city. As a result, they seem to feel that Southland Beach is becoming just another version of city life, perhaps intensified or exposed by peoples' nakedness or by the sun. Most say that it is common knowledge among Los Angeles County Lifeguards that in terms of social problems, Southland Beach is one of the two worst beaches in the entire county.

Most lifeguards are college-educated. They are not racists, nor even necessarily elitists. They are practical people who see change at Southland Beach and who worry about their role in this change. Most of them are also romantics who love something about the ocean and the sand. It is not surprising to learn that many guards prefer this beach in the winter, when it is sparkling, clear, and empty. Most would agree with a guard who said: "It's all these people. They really put hassles to your mind." Almost all lifeguards now agree that the beach is quite dangerous at night. Those who are on duty at headquarters at night lock all the doors and seldom sleep

well. Most think that North beach is not too dangerous during the day, but they believe that there are dangers on South
beach and around the pier even during the daytime. A few
guards will not permit their wives or children to come to
Southland Beach anymore, and the wife of one experienced
guard who used to enjoy sunbathing on North beach, has
been accosted by so many strange men that she now goes to
the gay beach farther north in order to be left alone.

Lifeguards love the beach environment, but they are increasingly distressed by the people who come to the beach
and bring social problems with them. Where these problems
are concerned, lifeguards readily admit their need for the
police. The reliance of lifeguards on police activity is necessary, as we shall see even more clearly in the next chapter. But
it would be a mistake to conclude that the lifeguards play only
a minor role in maintaining social order on the beach. First of
all, many beachgoers—including a majority of women—say
that they feel safe when they can see a lifeguard. Many of
these people say that they place their towels close to a
lifeguard tower to increase their security. On days when the
beach is largely deserted, some lifeguards will take it upon
themselves to ask women who are lying on the beach far from
a tower to move closer to it so that the lifeguard can protect
them. Second, a good many beachgoers go to a lifeguard
when they are in trouble. Whether the trouble is an injury, a
theft, or a sexual affront, people do go to the lifeguards for
help and help is usually forthcoming. Third, it is possible that
the presence of these lifeguards serves to deter some beach
problems. People familiar with the beach know that the
lifeguards can and will summon the police. How many
people who are unfamiliar with the beach know this, we cannot say; most whom we interviewed seemed not to know
about this possibility. Fourth, the direct intervention of
lifeguards in beach problems often prevents these conflicts
from escalating into something more serious. Direct intervention which leads to the arrest of someone for criminal activity
may deter future crime, not only by that person but by others

who witness the arrest. Finally, the lifeguards' telephone network permits them to bring the police to any part of the beach in short order. The resulting police activity may also have a deterring effect. Lifeguards on Southland Beach do more than protect public safety in the water; their presence and their activities help significantly to make the entire beach a place that beachgoers can think of as safe and pleasant.

# The Police

All of the Southland Beach is under the jurisdiction of the Southland City Police Department (SCPD). In 1975, when this research began, the SCPD consisted of 18 cadets (in training), 81 support personnel (secretaries, jailers, social workers, communications officers, etc.), and 113 police officers, 104 of whom are patrol officers, with the rest being sergeants or officers of higher rank. There was no appreciable change in personnel numbers in 1976. The SCPD maintains qualifications, salaries, and training comparable to that of larger metropolitan police forces, such as the Los Angeles Police Department, or the Los Angeles County Sheriff's Department, in whose academy their officers are trained. It has the most sophisticated communications equipment, as well as a helicopter and a fixed-wing aircraft which, unlike the noisy helicopter, can silently observe activity on the ground below.

The beach has posed a problem for the SCPD for a good many years. For one thing, the beach has long attracted many persons, including criminals, from many miles outside of Southland City. In fact, as we have seen, the overwhelming majority of all beachgoers lives outside Southland City. Now that a freeway empties directly onto the beach, it is more accessible for members of teenage gangs, criminals of all sorts, and transients. When such persons are joined at the beach by a large summer weekend crowd, the problems for the SCPD, who must also maintain order throughout the rest of Southland City, can become acute.

### Beach Patrol

Before 1974 the SCPD attempted to police the beach like any other part of the city, answering calls from beachgoers, merchants, or lifeguards by sending a radio-dispatched patrol car to the scene. Despite the direct telephone lines from lifeguard headquarters to the police, it would often take some time for a patrol car to arrive, and once the patrol car screeched to a stop in a parking lot or a nearby street, a police officer still had the awkward problem of crossing the sand to apprehend a suspect. Even the most athletic officer looked clumsy, if not comical, attempting to rush across soft sand while dressed in full uniform, including black leather shoes.

For this reason, and because the police, the lifeguards, and the Southland City Council believed that there was a growing crime problem on the beach (especially under the pier and just south of it), efforts were initiated to provide the police with a four-wheel drive, sand-tire equipped vehicle that could effectively patrol up and down the sand. After some delay, such a vehicle was purchased, painted with police identification, and put into service in the summer of 1974 as beach Unit 99. It continued in service throughout the period of this research in 1975 and 1976. Officers patrolling in this unit are armed with regulation revolver and baton, but they wear sneakers, short pants, and a white T-shirt marked with a police emblem. Thus, while they are identifiable as police officers, they can be as mobile on the sand as any suspect. In addition, a uniformed officer often patrolled the pier and promenade area along South beach on a three-wheel motor-cycle. Of course, patrol cars could still be called as needed.

In the summer of 1974, Unit 99 was usually manned during the day by both a police officer and a lifeguard. Most of the lifeguards disliked this assignment, and when the summer of 1975 began, Unit 99 was usually manned by a single police officer. During the summers of 1975 and 1976 several male officers and one female officer were regularly assigned to beach patrol in Unit 99, and others were regularly assigned to motorcycle patrol along the pier and promenade. The views and activities of these patrol officers add an important dimension to our understanding of social order at the beach.

### How Patrol Officers See the Beach

All of the Southland City police officers we spoke to or accompanied on patrol were cordial and cooperative. When we asked questions we felt that the answers given were thoughtful and frank, often surprisingly so. Perhaps our offer of anonymity was important, or perhaps these men and women were simply unusually independent. Whatever the reason, what they said followed no party line. On the contrary, they often expressed conflicting points of view. How they behaved also seemed to be unguarded; perhaps this is because the SCPD has a general policy of inviting citizens to "ride along" with officers on patrol and the officers have learned to behave "naturally" in the presence of these observers.

One beach patrol officer expressed the opinion that the police should not be patrolling the beach at all. He felt that the police are not needed during the day, although they are at night, and their uniformed presence only antagonizes beachgoers who "want to have a good time, not be watched by the police." Not surprisingly, he feels beachgoers' hostility as he patrols. In 1974 he and another officer became upset when two white teenage boys on the beach "oinked" at them. They shook the boys down, somewhat roughly, in an effort to command—or inspire—respect. The father of one of the boys was a prominent local citizen and his resulting complaint bruised feelings further. This officer also believes that the SCPD policy of citing citizens for bringing dogs to the beach is contrary to the spirit of the beach: "The beach and dogs go together." He thinks that beachgoers want to bring their dogs with them and that citing them is simply a means of providing revenue for the City. He believes also that most trouble on the beach is caused by people who do not live nearby. In his view, the beach during the winter is usually trouble-free, with trouble during the summer typically being only minor during the day. At night there is real trouble all year round he believes, and he says that he wouldn't come to the beach at night himself without a gun. His beach patrols, he feels, are largely uneventful. He cites dog owners, although he objects to the policy, and says that he could find marijuana on the beach any day he tried, but he doesn't bother since it causes no problems. Alcohol, however, does cause problems, and he watches for signs that drinkers are getting on other beachgoers' nerves. He is often called to pick up drunks who have wandered off the beach into nearby residential or business areas. Although he says that daylight crimes are almost always misdemeanors, he looks for persons who may be planning more serious crime after darkness falls. He seems to feel that he should be involved in more serious police work than is called for on the beach.

Another male officer believes that beach police patrol during the day is necessary, although he is if anything even more sympathetic to beachgoers and their right to enjoy themselves than the first officer was. He said that "people really have to work at it to screw up this beautiful environment, but somehow they manage." He strongly disagrees with the first officer by saying that daylight problems can be serious and that police presence is important not only in deterring such crime, but in being on the spot to react when crime occurs. Furthermore, he does not object to the dog citation policy, pointing out that dog feces on the hot sand lead to bacterial infections for beachgoers, because the sand cannot be properly sanitized to remove these bacteria. He agrees that some beachgoers want their dogs with them, but says that others object to dogs. He also agrees that most trouble on the beach is caused by non-local residents and that marijuana is not a problem, adding that smokers can always hide a "joint" in the sand, making apprehension impossible anyhow. He disagrees with the first officer about alcohol, however, saying that it is not a major problem, adding, "Besides I like to have

a beer on the beach myself." He, too, looks for serious offenses while he tries to "stay cool" and help beachgoers to
enjoy themselves. Unlike the first officer, he believes that
serious trouble does occur during the day and he is alert for
suspicious persons who might be present to victimize
beachgoers. For example, in addition to watching for addicts,
or thieves, he looks for homosexual men who might assault
children under the pier or bother other homosexual adults
who, he feels, have a perfect right to their way of life as long
as they confine their overt homosexuality to other adults in
private places. He is also different from the first officer because he feels no hostility from beachgoers, speaking instead
of warm and mutually respectful relations with regular
beachgoers, lifeguards, and local merchants. As we came to
observe, these people in turn, often speak well of him, and
behave toward him in a friendly fashion.

A third male officer tends to look at the beach as just
another part of the city where the law should be enforced.
Therefore he cites dog owners, looks for marijuana, and is
quite concerned about drinking. He often asks beachgoers,
particularly in large groups, to pour their beer or liquor out on
the sand if he feels they have the potential for getting "out of
control." He says that he does not cite these people if they
cooperate. He thinks that the presence of the mobile beach
patrol has been responsible for reducing crime on the beach
dramatically, saying that many serious troublemakers no
longer come to Southland Beach as a result. The summer of
1975, he feels, was remarkably trouble-free, although there
was still a problem with drinking and petty theft. Unlike the
other officers, he feels that there is more crime in the winter
than in the summer. He emphatically believes that the police
are needed on the beach but adds that they are not always
appreciated, and he is upset by the public hostility he sometimes feels.

A fourth officer, who is regularly on foot or motorcycle
patrol along the promenade, feels comfortable on the beach,
saying that for the most part he is accepted and liked, something which our observations confirm. He indicated that
three or four years ago the beach was seriously troubled by

violent crime. This is no longer the case, he believes, because of improved police patrol. He feels that the summer is far more troublesome than the winter, but that serious trouble occurs all year round. He agrees with the last officer that the beach requires police presence if crime is to be controlled, but he differs in believing that most beach crime is produced by "opportunistic" beachgoers themselves, not by outsiders.

A female officer sees the beach somewhat differently. She feels occasional hostility from beachgoers, saying that some people will taunt officers on the beach, sometimes even going so far as to throw sand at them. She says that there are some serious problems at the beach, more than beachgoers realize, in fact, but that she has never thought of it as being particularly dangerous during the day. When trouble does occur, she says, beachgoers seem to "tune out" and pay no attention. At night there are serious crimes of violence and the beach is quite dangerous. In her view, police patrol is necessary both day and night, but especially at night. She adds that despite her own feeling of ease on the beach, when she goes there off duty she is very worried about theft, and never takes anything with her but a towel and a dollar, not even any identification.

A final officer, also female, agreed that the beach was not a particularly dangerous place, saying that daytime crime primarily consists of theft or indecent exposure, with violent crimes occurring mainly at night. She believes that enforcing the laws against alcohol and marijuana would create more problems than it would solve. She also agreed that most beachgoers do not notice what is going on around them because they believe that nothing unpleasant will happen to them. She added that she and most SCPD personnel who know about what can happen at Southland Beach no longer go there themselves for pleasure: "It isn't that our beach is worse than any other beach, but when you work there and know what goes on, you don't feel safe because you know the potential dangers."

The most obvious conclusion one can draw from these opinions is that experienced beach patrol officers disagree about how dangerous a place this beach really is. Some think that it is quite dangerous, others that it is quite safe. All agree that the beach is more dangerous south of the pier than north, and that the pier itself attracts many dangerous persons, but the amount and nature of the danger is seen somewhat differently by each officer. And, as these officers themselves agree, how a police officer reacts to crime on the beach involves matters of personality as well as past experiences.

Because in any police work both the perception of crime and the response to it so often involves the discretion of the patrol officer, it is important to recognize that officers differ in how they feel about the beach and in how they react to trouble when it occurs.[1] Furthermore, as these officers also realize, officers may react differently from one day to the next. In order to get a sense of how police officers actually cope with problems on Southland Beach, the author or a female research associate rode along with various police officers in Unit 99 on fourteen separate occasions in 1975 and 1976.[2]

### Patrolling the Beach in Unit 99

On a cool, somewhat overcast weekday in August, a female member of the research staff rode along with a male officer on a full day's beach patrol. The first problem to be encountered occurred about 9:30 A.M. when the officer stopped Unit 99 next to a shabby middle-aged man who was lying on the sand. The officer peered at him then said with relief, "He's moving," and drove on; he had been fearful that the man might have been dead. Several other sleeping bodies were examined in the next few minutes; all were alive. Nothing else of interest was encountered along the largely deserted sand until 10:30 A.M., when at the extreme southern end of the beach Unit 99 pulled alongside a woman who was sleeping on the sand next to an old suitcase and rolled up coat. She said she was from the Netherlands, and since she was a tourist and did not appear to be disoriented, drunk, or high on drugs, the officer drove on without filling out a field interrogation (FI) report (a report filed by most police departments concerning suspicious activity).

By this time people were beginning to arrive on the beach. As the patrol drove north, two young girls waved at the police vehicle from their position near a lifeguard tower; one waved her hand, the other playfully waved her bikini top. As the vehicle approached, the topless girl coyly dressed. The vehicle drove on and the officer stopped to talk to lifeguards, beach merchants, or beachgoers whom he recognized. Nothing of consequence happened until 11:30 A.M., when a surfer who was no more than 13 years old flagged down Unit 99 saying that two young men had stolen his lunch and his money—45 cents. One of the men escaped in a car, whose license the boy reported, while the other was still in sight walking across a parking lot. After calling in the information, the officer pursued the suspect as far as he could in his vehicle, then jumped out and ran after him, climbing up stairs onto the pier. After a ten-minute pursuit, he returned without seeing the suspect again.

As the vehicle resumed its patrol, this time down the promenade, four women on bicycles dismounted and waved. They asked if they would get a ticket for riding their bikes since a nearby sign read "No bike riding." They were told that they would not, since SCPD policy is to ignore this ordinance in favor of keeping people happy. After a thirty-minute break for lunch at the police station, the patrol resumed. The beach crowd was now much larger and the sun was starting to come out. A teenage couple with a dog was stopped at 12:40 P.M. They were told to get the dog off the beach, but were not cited since the officer decided that they were not local people and might not have seen the signs prohibiting dogs. A few moments later, another couple with a dog was stopped with the same result. At 12:50 P.M. a lifeguard flagged down the unit to ask the officer to call out of the water two young women, who had been swimming out too far and had refused the lifeguard's order to come in. At the moment, they were gaily waving their bikini tops in the air. The officer used his loudspeaker to tell them to come in, "preferably with your tops on." (This was not really his preference, he confided.) Two kids with a puppy were stopped next and told that their puppy was cute, but that it was not allowed on the beach. Shortly thereafter the smell of marijuana wafted by and the vehicle turned quickly toward an adult male, fully dressed, who promptly buried his joint in the sand. The officer said, "Thank you." and turned his vehicle away.

Now that the beach was becoming crowded, it was more difficult to drive along the sand; the officer was often forced to change course to avoid hitting people. At 1:20 P.M. there was a radio call for assistance from a police officer on the promenade. When Unit 99 arrived after a short drive from North beach, the officer who called pointed out a young woman who was lying on the grass. She was dishevelled and disoriented. After she failed to answer the most elementary questions about herself, the day, the date, or even the year, the two officers agreed to take her to a nearby mental health clinic. They led her gently to the vehicle, but suddenly she screamed and kicked, shouting "Help, what are you doing? I want my father!" The officers finally got her into the vehicle and dropped her off at the clinic.

Unit 99 returned to the beach, where a lifeguard signaled to the vehicle saying that two teenaged girls nearby had complained that a middle-aged black man had exposed himself to them. The officer drove over to the man and said without sarcasm, "I hear you're having some problems with your trunks." As the conversation progressed, the officer filled out an FI, learning as he did so that the man worked as a mental health counselor in another Southern California city. The man claimed that his zipper kept falling down, and asked the officer if he should leave the beach. The officer politely and tactfully asked him what he thought, and the man decided that he should leave because of his faulty trunks. The officer then spoke to the Chicano family whose daughters had complained, asking them what happened. The girls said in English that they had been scared. The officer asked what had happened: "Did it fall out?" They said, "No, he took it out." The officer later explained that even had the girls pressed the complaint, which they chose not to do, the circumstances were so ambiguous that a conviction was highly unlikely. He added that he hoped the man would not soon return.

There was no further trouble until shortly after 3:00 P.M., when Unit 99 was called concerning a fight that was taking place in a shabby rooming house that fronted on the promenade near the pier. Unit 99 drove to the scene as rapidly as the crowd permitted and the officer rushed into the dimly lighted hallway, meeting a longhaired young man who said "there's blood all over." A confused interrogation followed in which several newly arrived officers from patrol cars queried three young men who said that a girl had been raped and they had been protecting her. Another young man with a bloody and battered face was accused of the rape. He denied it. The girl, it seems, was nowhere to be found. The men were quite intoxicated, but managed to say that they were from out-of-state. One of these men who was already known to the police was arrested for drunkenness. The others were released while the investigation continued (some days later, the woman in question did file a rape complaint). This interchange took about 45 minutes, most of which was spent comparing the men's stories, listening to bystanders, searching the rooming house, and looking for the girl. By the time the arrest was completed, it was 4:30 P.M. and the beach patrol was turned over to another officer.

This patrol illustrates several important features of the Unit 99 beach patrol. First, mornings are relatively trouble-free and patrolling is usually more or less continuous. The officer may in fact have to look for something to do to occupy the time. As the day warms and a crowd gathers, patrolling is more difficult, and trouble is more likely. A problem such as that presented by the man who exposed himself can occupy an officer for 15 or 20 minutes; investigating the alleged rape took almost two hours. During the time the officer in Unit 99 is occupied, he cannot patrol, and any visual deterrent value the unit may have on the beach is lost; similarly, the officer is not available to detect crime elsewhere on the beach.

To look further at the problems of afternoon patrolling, another weekday ride in Unit 99, this time by the author, is illustrative. The July day was warm and sunny at noon when the patrol began, but the beach was not yet very crowded. The unit patrolled rapidly up and down the beach, zigzag-

ging from the wet sand near the water to the soft sand and
back again. Five people with dogs were stopped. All were
told to remove their dogs, but none was cited. This was probably because all were out-of-towners. One man from Ohio
became sarcastic and was told sharply to get his dog off the
beach "right now." This man was watched closely to be certain that he followed the order. During the first hour of patrol, the unit was asked twice to meet the "animal control"
vehicle, which lacks four-wheel drive, to assist them in picking up a stray dog. Once, two animal control officers hitched
a ride on Unit 99 to a lifeguard tower to pick up a pelican that
had been found dead with its throat cut. Amid ghoulish
comments from the lifeguards about Jack the Ripper, the bird
was thrown into the vehicle and taken back to the animal
control vehicle.

Although the crowd had increased considerably, there
were no other incidents until 2:00 P.M., when two teenaged
boys ran up to Unit 99 to say that their surfboard had just
been stolen and they had seen it being taken away in a car.
The officer quickly called for police units to intercept the car,
but when he learned that neither of the boys was the owner
of the board (both were friends of the owner who was said to
be off in pursuit of the thief), he said that he would return
later to take a report when the owner had come back. As it
happened, he was too busy to return, so this potential theft
statistic was lost to the record. As he drove on looking for the
boy whose surfboard had been taken, a call came over the
radio to watch for a Caucasian male, aged about 25, who was
thought still to be in the area, and to be carrying a shotgun in
a sleeping bag. Despite much looking, this suspect was not
seen, much to the relief of the civilian passenger.

At 2:30 P.M., while patrolling the promenade to the south,
the officer spotted something and swung quickly over a curb
to drive to a nearby apartment house. He had seen the car of a
man who was wanted for rape. He parked, called other officers and together they moved in on the house where they
found not the rapist, but a friend of his. In all, the approach
and interrogation took half an hour. Returning to the beach

and patrolling north along the promenade near the pier, a young, modishly dressed Englishwoman hailed the unit. The officer listened politely as she told him of having her purse stolen when she momentarily set it down on the pier. He began to take a routine report until the woman said that the amount taken was $4000 in cash. At this he visibly started, his attitude changing from concern to suspicion. That amount of money—in cash—was indeed unusual. The resulting investigation involved six officers who looked all around the pier and under it without effect, even though a black employee of one place identified some young blacks as suspects. No one was arrested and no money was recovered, even though the suspects (who were FI'd) were discreetly followed for more than an hour with the help of the SCPD aircraft, which continually radioed their movements to a patrol car, hoping that the boys would lead officers to the stolen money. The officers left believing that the victim—the wife of an English rock musician who also made an appearance—was probably attempting to buy cocaine, and that despite their failure to find the thieves, justice may indirectly have been done. This investigation consumed two hours. By the time the officer from Unit 99 returned to the police station and filed his report, the day was over. As a result, anything that happened after 2:30 P.M. on the beach would have been invisible to Unit 99.

Another afternoon patrol, this time on a reasonably crowded Sunday, gives us another perspective. The patrol once again began at noon, with the author as observer. At 12:10 P.M. Unit 99 told a food truck driver that he would have to leave the beach because he was doing business without a license. At 12:25 P.M. three adults with a puppy were asked if the dog belonged to them; the officer was told that it did not, only to see one of the men call the dog and head for his car. The officer drove to the car and confronted the man with his lie. The man first attempted to laugh it off saying with heavy sarcasm, "Are you going to give me a ticket? Aw, please Mr. Lifeguard, sir, don't give me a ticket!" The officer answered, "Yes, I'm going to give you a ticket and its not Mr. Lifeguard, sir, it's Mr. Police Officer." The young man was visibly shocked and apologetic. Asked for his identification, the man went to his car and the officer, who followed him, unholstered his service revolver. When the man emerged from the car with the ID, rather than a weapon of his own, the gun was holstered and the citation was written. A few minutes later the officer sighed, and said, "this is the part of the job I hate," referring to unholstering his gun, something which is called for by police procedures.

As Unit 99 drove south along the beach, two teenaged boys ran up to it saying that some kids were beating them up. As they pointed to their laughing assailants it became clear the boys were joking and the officer dismissed them good-naturedly. At 12:45 P.M. a man who had a Doberman on a leash was stopped. When the officer began to cite him, he became abusive referring to the officer's "quota" and asking, "Are you trying to make points with the boss?" The officer wrote the citation politely, pointing out later that the man clearly knew he was violating the law because he had referred to the fact that no sign forbidding dogs was visible at that point on the beach, clearly indicating that he was aware of such signs and of the law.

Ten minutes later a middle-aged man flagged Unit 99 down and said that "this punk kid," pointing to a blond 13-year-old boy, was "giving a lady a bad time" by using obscene language. The officer called the boy over and told him to "cool it," adding that if there were further trouble he'd have to leave the beach. No record of this kind of trouble is made unless there is a citation or an FI. Neither was issued. A moment later the officer used his loudspeaker to tell a sailboat to move farther out, that it was getting too close to the beach. A lifeguard later thanked him for doing so.

At 1:20 P.M. Unit 99 was called off the beach to take a drunken man to the station. After 20 minutes, the vehicle returned and began to patrol North beach. A man with a large German Shepherd was told to remove the dog. The officer stopped to check a men's restroom for homosexual behavior. Nothing was noticed. At 2:20 P.M. a large number of Chicano adults awkwardly attempted to hide their beer cans as the unit drove by. The officer said nothing. Just at this point a girl stopped the vehicle to tell the officer that she had found a lost child, a little boy of three or four. The officer took the child, checked the lifeguard reports for lost children and finding none, drove up and down the sand hoping that the boy would point out his mother. The unit was soon flagged down by the boy's mother, who said that she knew all along where her child was and thought the police officer was only being nice by giving him a ride. The officer was polite but annoyed: "Does she think that all I have to do is give joy rides to little kids?" Shortly thereafter two black families were seen illegally cooking on barbeques. The officer rhetorically said, "What am I supposed to do, tell them they can't have lunch?" and drove on.

At 2:45 P.M. Unit 99 received an "officer needs assistance" call from a street near the promenade. With the siren turned on, Unit 99 rushed to the location to find two women, one white and one black, fighting in the street. The police officer present could not subdue the women without help or the use of physical force, and it finally took several officers to force one of the women into a patrol car. The woman was intoxicated and later attempted to tear a jail cell apart; the fight was said by onlookers to have been a lover's quarrel.

Returning to the beach at 3:10 P.M., the officer saw the same German Shepherd and approached it. A white woman of about 30 rushed up and said, "Don't take him, that's my dog." She next said that she was only taking care of the dog for a friend. The officer began to fill out a citation and the woman became quite upset. Her girlfriend now arrived and told her not to answer any questions and to walk away. This the woman did, saying "I don't have to answer anything." The officer politely but firmly grabbed her wrist and held her, telling her that she had to remain. She began to twist away and screamed abuse at him. A crowd gathered, including eventually the dog's owner, who turned out to be an attorney who threatened to sue the officer for "abusive behavior."

After much railing and recrimination, the woman signed the citation and Unit 99 drove away with the attorney yelling after it, "I'll take you to court."

During this altercation, the lifeguard called to say that he had received four complaints about a "drunk woman" near his tower on South beach. The woman was with three men, and all were foreign-speaking with heavy, indeterminable accents. When Unit 99 arrived, and the officer approached the woman, she complained about police harassment and insisted that she was not drunk, even though she staggered and almost fell when she tried to stand up. The officer quietly cautioned these people, filled out an FI on the woman's husband, and told them that they would have to leave the beach if there were any further complaints.

Passing the Chicano family with the beer once again, the officer told them not to drink on the beach, but drove away without further action. At 4:05 P.M. a Spanish-speaking woman reported that her purse containing $149 in cash had been stolen from her car, but a bystander said that a Spanish-speaking girl had the purse and was trying to find the owner. A crime report was filled out and the woman was given phone numbers to call in case the purse had been turned in.

Shortly thereafter a couple was stopped and cited for having their dog on the beach. They were polite, and asked for a warning instead of a ticket, but were told—politely—that the signs were the warning. Driving north, another dog was seen and it was none other than the German Shepherd that had caused so much trouble. With help from a friendly beachgoer, the dog was put in the vehicle, and as Unit 99 drove away, a man rushed up shouting "That's my friend's dog." He was told that the friend could pick it up at the pound. Leaving the beach, two more barbeques were seen but ignored. After dropping off the dog at the pound, it was necessary to fill out a long report on the incident with the German Shepherd, and Unit 99 did not return to the beach until later in the evening.

It seems obvious that the frequent afternoon involvements of Unit 99 which take it away from routine patrol restrict its effectiveness as a means of deterring crime or apprehending criminals. As we have already seen, the discretion of individual officers also affects records—one offender becomes a crime statistic, another walks away with a warning. All officers encounter citizens who rub them the wrong way, transforming what the officer had originally thought of as a warning into a confrontation that often leads to a citation, sometimes even to an arrest. The citizen's attitude is important in these equations. The officer's attitude is also important, as in the following example in which a person who was likely to become a crime statistic got off with a warning.

During a brief ride with Unit 99 an episode of some considerable mayhem was witnessed. Two women were fighting tooth and nail on the sand. One was an Anglo woman in her fifties, the other an American Indian woman in her mid-twenties. An older man and small boy were watching. When the officer drove up next to them, the women stopped the combat and began to complain. He listened, deftly cooling them off while at the same time extracting information about them and their quarrel. It finally emerged that the older woman loves to feed seagulls and on this occasion was doing so when an eight-year-old boy began to chase them. She called him a "damn devil," asking him "Would you want someone to do that when you're eating?" His mother, the Indian woman, defended him by physically attacking the older woman. The police officer quickly determined that the Indian woman had initiated the attack and was quite intoxicated as well. Saying, "O.K., nobody's hurt," the officer told the Indian woman to leave the beach. The older woman complained, asking "Is she black or what?" He answered, "Remember one thing, the color doesn't matter. It's just her personality." The officer later explained that he did not want to take the Indian woman to jail, although she was guilty of assault, because of the boy. He hoped that the mother would sober up, and the boy would be better off this way. He also felt that the older woman had not been injured and little harm had been done. Another officer—or this one on another day—might have arrested the woman for assault.

To emphasize these problematic features of police work on Southland Beach, let us look at one more beach patrol which the author observed on a very warm, crowded Sunday in early August 1976. When the patrol began at 1:00 P.M., the officer was about to head north toward County Beach, where the Los Angeles Police Department was preparing to make arrests on the so-called "gay" beach. Because these arrests were expected to cause resistance and perhaps even precipitate a riot among the gay men, Unit 99 was standing by. This tense situation was the result of a confrontation on the previous Fourth of July, when two undercover LAPD officers attempted to arrest two nude gay men who had allegedly been engaged openly in oral intercourse on this beach. Before the arrest could be made, a large crowd of gay men surrounded the two officers and threatened violence; Unit 99 rushed to the rescue and managed to save the situation before serious violence erupted. This was possible because of an earlier intelligence report that violence was expected on the beach that July 4, and that a militant group might attempt to kill a police officer on the sand. There were two officers in Unit 99. Both wore riot helmets, carried shotguns, and were provided with extra ammunition. Their equipment and manner had intimidated the crowd. Now, several weeks later, Unit 99 was watching and its lone officer, in beach uniform, was hoping that a repetition of the Fouth of July could be avoided. He monitored the LAPD operation until 3:00 P.M., when the planned arrest was made without any intervention by the crowd. Because of the necessity to maintain surveillance of this potential riot, no routine patrols were made between 1:00 and 3:00 P.M., but when patrol was resumed, there was never a dull moment.

First, there was an amplified rock band on the sand, something which was clearly illegal. The officer said he would have dealt with it earlier but he was too busy trying to monitor the progress of the potentially dangerous riot. As he drove past this area at 3:00 P.M., even though the band had stopped playing, a woman called to him and asked if he were not going to do something about the noise since she and

others came to the beach "to relax and have things quiet."
The officer said he agreed completely and felt that way himself and said this would be a good time to talk to the band
members who were then packing up their gear. He talked to
them very politely and pleasantly, telling them that it was
illegal to have amplified music on the beach, adding that
since they were leaving he would merely wish them on their
way, but warning them not to play there again. They agreed
and left without complaint.

The patrol continued when to the observer's surprise the
officer pulled Unit 99 over next to a young Anglo man walking on the sand away from the hotdog stand; the officer said
in a quiet voice, "Can't you do something about your trunks
to make them a little more decent so that everything isn't
hanging out?" The young man looked down and said, "Oh,
yeah, my God, thank you," in an embarrassed way, saying
that he had not intended to expose himself in that manner. In
any event, this was the end of the episode and the young
man was not seen again.

A few minutes later, well back on the sand behind tower
15, the officer again swerved the car. What he had seen, at
some distance away, were two apparently gay men, one of
whom was naked, on the sand. As Unit 99 drove up, the
naked man was lying on his side, the other one was sitting
up; the officer said to the one who was sitting up, "Hey,
would you tell your partner to get some clothes on?" The man
looked flustered, and said nothing so the officer harshly
added: "Just get some pants on him and keep them on him."
Without issuing a citation the officer drove away, muttering
something under his breath that sounded like "animals."

In this same area a minute later, two black women came
running over and said "Officer, this little boy is lost." The
child was a four-year-old Chicano boy who wouldn't say anything but his first name. The officer very kindly and warmly
took the little boy over to the lifeguard tower, walking him by
the hand, and left him with the lifeguard. Only a minute later
he stopped to help a young black man, who complained
about being unable to get his car backed out of the parking

lot. The car was a very large old Chevrolet and it did not appear to be blocked; instead it seemed that the man could not drive the car very well. With great courtesy, the officer directed him when to cut the wheel and so forth, and helped him out with no trouble, saying later, that such problems often happen when women can't get their cars out, and in those cases he drives the car for them, but since this time it was a man he didn't want to embarrass him by taking the wheel away from him. A moment later, still in the parking lot, he yelled at three Chicanos to "get your buddy out of sight" since the young man was staggering drunk, but the officer again did nothing about citing or arresting the youngster for public drunkenness.

Unit 99 next drove to the promenade area, and we parked by a lemonade stand. It immediately became obvious that this officer had a great many friends in the area, whom he greeted warmly and who returned his greetings with equal enthusiasm. Unlike the situation on the sandy beach where some people stare at Unit 99 with surprise, on the promenade it seems to be taken for granted; no one stares at it even though in that crowded area it seems to be a very large official vehicle. There was a clear sense of the officer belonging there. Before we could buy some lemonade, a woman of about thirty-five came rushing over to the officer, pointing out her cut knees and a bruise on her arm, insisting that her "boyfriend," who runs a refreshment stand on the promenade, had broken into her apartment, beaten her up, and had taken from her the keys to her apartment which she kept on a chain around her neck. The officer took her aside, talked to her for some time and said he would talk to the man involved. He then spoke softly and discreetly to the man, who denied that there had been a fight, and denied knowing anything about the keys. Back outside, the officer explained to the woman that he couldn't forcibly search her friend for the keys, and there really wasn't much he could do unless she wanted to swear out an assault complaint against him, which at this point she did not want to do. She was told to think it over and to file a complaint in the morning if she wished. She agreed, and the officer put his arm around her and walked her along the promenade, calming her noticeably. He seemed to be handling things skillfully; indeed, it was difficult to imagine anyone doing better.

Ten minutes later it was apparent that all his skill had not been enough, however, because the woman had gone back, seen her boyfriend and once again he had allegedly refused to give her the keys. Now she was crying, demanding the keys to her apartment, and lamenting everything endlessly. In fact, she now wanted to swear out a complaint. The officer listened, then fumbled around for a form, saying that he didn't have the right one, so he just wrote her name and some details of her complaint on a plain piece of paper. He was almost certainly stalling for time hoping that the woman would drop the matter if he took no immediate action. This domestic squabble took almost 30 minutes of Unit 99's time; yet had the officer not taken the action he did, violence could easily have resulted.

As soon as the domestic tiff was calmed, calls began coming in about a fight at tower 25 on South beach. By the time Unit 99 arrived, the fight was over, but it was described by an excited lifeguard who explained that an exceptional series of events had taken place near his tower in the last few minutes. First, it seems that a young Anglo man threw a frisbee which hit another young man who was lying down. The person hit by the frisbee got up and punched the frisbee thrower, blackening and closing his eye. The injured man came to the lifeguard station for first aid; the lifeguards asked if he wanted to swear out a complaint, but since it was obvious to them that he was "on drugs," they were not surprised when he did not want to make a complaint and simply left the beach saying, "No, that's cool man, forget it." A few minutes after that, a black man was seen exposing himself, whether intentionally or not could not really be determined, but there was a complaint about it from a woman, and a lifeguard went over and asked him to please put his "parts" back into his pants or he would call the police. The man did as requested, and then left the beach. A few minutes after that a fight started in the parking lot behind the tower involving a number of teenagers of various ethnic groups, and a crowd gathered to watch. No one intervened and the fight broke up before the police could get there.

The lifeguard attributed these occurrences to the growing use of Quaalude or other drugs in the area, saying that "everyone was doped out of their minds" that day. After learning about these events, which had taken place while the domestic quarrel was being cooled off, the officer drove back to North beach to make a final check on the riot area. He had just reached the edge of County Beach when he received another call from tower 25, this time saying that a ten-year-old boy had been lost since 11:30 A.M. in the morning and it was now almost 5:00 P.M.. By the time Unit 99 drove all the way back to South beach, lifeguards had just found the boy, who, it was said, had been in the water for five and a half hours. The boy was as round and sleek as a young porpoise, so perhaps he could have been in the water that long.

As Unit 99 drove away, an Anglo man at the waterline was seen digging a huge hole which kids were jumping into. The officer called out to him on the loudspeaker, "Sir, for the safety of the children and this vehicle, would you please fill in the hole right away, preferably without the children in it?"

### The Police and Southland Beach

We have seen that the police officers who patrol Southland Beach have varied beliefs and attitudes about crime on the beach, and that their actual approach to beach patrol differs as well. What is more, the same officer will patrol differently from one day to the next; in fact, an officer's approach to patrolling may change dramatically over the course of a single day. These differences and changes will be of particular significance to us later, when we try to assess police records about crime on Southland Beach.

These differences are important, to be sure, but so are certain consistencies of summer beach patrol that are present regardless of individual differences between officers. Thus when the beach crowd is small, as is the case on most weekday mornings and on some cool, overcast afternoons, there is little trouble and officers often must look for something to do. But during warm afternoons or on weekends, when the crowd is large, Unit 99 cannot possibly cope with more than a fraction of the trouble that occurs on the beach, the parking lots, and the promenade. At such times, many problems that might well receive considerable attention on a quiet morning go unattended while the harried officer in Unit 99 does his or her best to deal with the most pressing problems of the moment.

Our research has indicated, as the next chapter will document, that a beachgoer who spends the day lying on the sand at Southland Beach is not likely to encounter serious trouble, even on a very crowded day. For example, during the hours of the Sunday afternoon patrol just described, when Unit 99 was overwhelmed by one sort of trouble or another, three research associates carefully observed the beach behavior visible to them near lifeguard towers 8, 16, and 15. These observers saw only a few minor violations of beach rules or ordinances, and nothing at all serious was witnessed.

From the perspective of an ordinary beachgoer, then, it was possible to experience such a day as altogether safe and pleasant. From the perspective of the police officer in Unit 99, however, the day was a three-ring circus with far more trouble occurring than he could conceivably cope with. We will examine these contrasting perspectives later. For now, we want to emphasize that however much officers may appear to differ in their beliefs about crime on Southland Beach, on crowded days they all must face far more trouble than they can handle. Since most afternoons and all weekends during the summer are crowded, it is obvious why the Southland City Police Department considers keeping the peace on this beach to be a major problem. Let us now examine what the beach looks like from the beachgoers' perspective.

# 5

## Trouble at the Beach: Direct Observations of Beachgoers

At the very beginning of this research, in June and July 1975, over one hundred hours were spent on Southland Beach in informal observation and conversation, which was intended to provide a record of differences and similarities among beachgoers all along the beach. By the use of traditional ethnographic procedures such as participant observation and informal interviews, we sought to determine for each portion of the beach when crowds arrived, how they were typically constituted, how they ordinarily behaved, and what kinds of things happened that annoyed or alarmed them. Casual conversations on many topics were also held with lifeguards, fishermen, parking lot attendants, merchants, and passersby on the promenade.[1]

After these preliminary investigations, three observers (the author and two women assistants) began more focused observations along the beach in order to refine observational methods and make certain that inter-observer reliability could be achieved. The purpose of these observations was not to record subtle features of interaction, such as exact distances between beachgoers on the sand, details of their non-verbal behavior, or the precise nature of their conversations. For one thing, the noise of the surf and the sea breeze usually made it impossible to overhear conversations unless voices were raised, but even had it been possible and ethical to eavesdrop, the purposes of this study made a fine-grained record of conversation or behavior unnecessary. Instead, our interest was in more obvious, easily observed aspects of behavior, the kinds of occurrences that stood out so clearly that they could be seen at a distance and agreed upon by independent observers.

Accordingly, we began our systematic program of observation by defining a study area, usually a rectangle of some 30 to 50 yards along the beach front and as many yards inland as the observer was able to monitor given the conditions of crowding. On days when the beach was only sparsely crowded it was often possible to see everything of relevance all the way from the waterline to the rear wall of the beach; on crowded days, there were so many beachgoers to be watched that it was difficult to record behaviors farther than 30 or 40 yards inland. Once the study area was set, we recorded the location, sex, age, ethnicity, and pairing of people in the area (for example, "male alone," "male-female couple," "parents with two four- to six-year old children"), then watched to see what kinds of rule violations might occur. We also recorded the reactions of beachgoers to these violations. We were not concerned with recording everything people did—sitting, sleeping, talking, playing cards, and the like. Instead we were interested in two classes of phenomena: first, obvious rule violations, and second, trouble, whether the trouble was related to an obvious rule violation or not. Trouble, as defined earlier, is the term we used to refer to evidence that one person visibly took offense at the behavior of another.

We recorded violations of three kinds of rules: (1) commonly understood laws (for example, laws against theft, assault, and indecent exposure); (2) municipal ordinances governing beach behavior (no fires, no alcoholic beverages, and no dogs, for details see Chapter Two); and (3) certain "beach rules" that seemed to be widely understood by beachgoers (such as not placing one's towel too close to another party, not throwing frisbees too close to sleeping per-

sons, and not kicking sand on others by running past them).
It was not difficult to record all or almost all rule violations of
general laws or beach ordinances. On a crowded day, however, it was sometimes difficult to record all the violations of
the presumed beach rules. Inter-judge reliabilities regarding
violations of laws and ordinances ran well above .90, but the
agreement concerning the violations of beach rules could fall
as low as .50 depending on the size of the crowd and the
nature of the rule.

The second category of interest was "trouble" which was
observable when someone displayed obvious anger, complained loudly or asked for an account ("Watch it," "What do
you think you're doing?" "Can't you be more careful?"),
quickly picked up personal belongings and moved away, engaged in open confrontation (shouting, shoving), or made a
formal complaint to a lifeguard or a police officer. It was only
sometimes possible to determine to what extent someone was
upset, offended, or annoyed, and such judgments were not
regularly attempted. Thus a number of offenses that did not
lead to clearly visible signs of trouble but did produce fear or
annoyance undoubtedly went unrecorded. When trouble was
visible it was usually, but not always, possible to determine
what rule violation had triggered it, or at least what rule
violation ostensibly did so.

Conditions at Southland Beach allow observations such as
these to be made with considerable accuracy. The behaviors
being recorded were clearly visible, and because it was possible to observe on the beach for long periods of time without
exciting anyone's interest, there was little reason to fear that
the process of observation was itself affecting the behavior
being observed. This point is important. Our preliminary
ethnographic investigations indicated that someone who
dressed like an ordinary beachgoer could sit or lie on the
beach, look around discreetly, and take notes without arous-
ing curiosity. Glancing at others is a common and acceptable
feature of beach life, and many beachgoers, especially men,
glance at other people on the beach continually. Writing is
also common, and many people on the beach write letters,

pausing from time to time to look around. It is even possible to take photographs of others on this beach without anyone seeming to take notice.

Throughout hundreds of hours of observation and recording we received no complaints. There were only a handful of queries about note taking, and since these were invariably made to a female observer by a male beachgoer, it is reasonable to assume that the note taking was merely a convenient topic chosen by men in order to initiate a conversation with an attractive woman. On no occasion was a beachgoer noticed to move away from an observer, nor were there any complaints about us which we overheard, or which were passed on to us by lifeguards. The process of observation, then, was a natural part of the beach scene. The result of these observations appears to be an accurate, non-reactive record of observable violations of beach ordinances or well-known laws, and of the visible kinds of trouble that sometimes follow. It is a less accurate record of violations of various beach rules, and it is an unreliable record of how beachgoers felt about the behavior that we saw going on about them.[2]

The accuracy of these observations will be more easily evaluated when the observations themselves are presented and discussed, but a few examples here may be helpful. On a warm, sunny weekday observations were made by two persons for two hours. The area studied was 65 yards wide, from the berm to a point about 100 yards inland. The study area contained 63 people as observations began. This number remained steady throughout the period of observation; some people left the beach, but a similar number of new arrivals replaced them. There were 10 single men, mostly in their twenties or thirties, three single women in their early twenties, and five couples; there was one group of two men, two of two women, another of four women, three of three women, and one of six teenage males. There was one woman with a child, another group of three women with one child, a group of two young men and two young women, and another of two teenage males with one teenage girl.

During two hours of observation the following rules were

violated: (1) several dogs ran on the beach; (2) a frisbee almost hit a young woman, landing between her legs while she sat writing something; (3) a young woman who took her toddler to wade in the water had both breasts fall out of her bikini top, and she made no effort to replace them for about 30 seconds; (4) this same woman later breastfed her child while talking to passersby at the waterline; and (5) the necking of a teenage couple became so passionate that sexual intercourse was almost consummated on the sand.

While both observers agreed in recording these occurrences as rule violations, it was also noted that only two of the violations led to anything that could be considered even mildly annoying. First, the girl who was almost hit by a frisbee looked startled, but handed the frisbee back without obvious anger or comment. Second, the teenage couple's necking became so passionate, and involved such overt petting, that several nearby beachgoers stared in open amazement, then looked either embarrassed or angered. No one left the area, however. We would conclude that one beach ordinance (the dogs) was violated several times, and four common beach rules were also violated; we would also conclude that only very slight "trouble" was seen.

As this two-hour period illustrates, rule violations themselves are usually reasonably easy to observe—there is a dog on the beach, someone is drinking beer, someone is exposing himself. "Trouble," on the other hand, is a gloss for a complex process which often can be observed only in part. For example, in response to some kind of an offense, anger may be felt but not expressed; and if it is expressed its initial flare-up may be missed, or the outcome may be lost altogether because the participants move away. The following example illustrates this problem. At a location on South beach before 11:00 A.M. on an exceptionally hot sunny day, an observer recorded, among other things, a sequence of drinking behavior that lasted over an hour and a half. When the observer arrived and defined a 35 by 45 yard study area, she noticed a group of seven males aged 13-15 who were engaged in drinking vodka or gin out of plastic cups. The violation was obvious: alcoholic beverages are illegal on Southland Beach, and these boys were clearly under age. As time passed, several of the boys became boisterous, shouting obscenities and throwing sand at one another. The sand almost hit several people nearby, but only one of these looked up in annoyance and no one said anything. Indeed, a nearby group of adults laughed, apparently amused by the youngsters' increasingly drunken antics. After an hour and a half, one of the boys lay prostrate on the sand, apparently quite intoxicated. Two lifeguards then approached the group of youngsters and told them to take showers and get off the beach. Whether the order reflected a concern for the law or for the danger of heat stroke on such a hot day could not be determined. After giving their order, the lifeguards left but the boys neither took showers nor departed. After a few minutes the lifeguards returned and ordered the boys to put water on the intoxicated boy's face. They then joined the boys in dragging the most intoxicated boy into the shade under the lifeguard tower. Another 45 minutes passed and the police did not arrive, a delay which means that no call to them was placed. The heat of the day forced the observer (who had to remain in the sun) to leave before the boys left the area.

The problem here is that while the occurrence of a rule violation was obvious, trouble was not. Only one person seemed to be annoyed. No one actually complained, and the lifeguards were apparently more concerned with the health of the teenagers than with law enforcement. Yet due to the forced departure of the observer, the outcome of the episode was not determined. We can only surmise that while the law was flagrantly broken, no one was particularly bothered by it. We cannot be certain, however, that some more serious trouble did not occur before the boys finally left the beach.

We rarely interviewed either participants or witnesses concerning the rule violations or trouble that we witnessed during these periods of observation because we were primarily concerned with recording the frequency of occurrence of rule violation and trouble, not with details concerning process, and we felt that by stopping to interview people we would lose sight of everything else that might occur while the interview was taking place. We also avoided such interviews because we did not want to risk influencing anyone by suggesting to them, however inadvertently, that they should be upset by something that they might otherwise have taken lightly.[3]

### Results of the Observational Study

It was the consensus of police and lifeguard opinion as well as our own ethnographic investigations that the highest frequency of trouble on Southland Beach occurs in the area just south of the pier around lifeguard tower 16, and just north of it at tower 15. For this reason, we centered a series of observations on these two areas as well as on various so-called "Anglo" areas on the beach, where trouble was said to be less frequent (for example, County Beach, towers 8–11, and towers 24–27). Following the procedures discussed before, in 1975 three observers made 30 hours of observation; half of these focused on areas 15 and 16 with the rest being divided among the other areas. All observations were made between 10 A.M. and 4 P.M., with the majority centered in the peak crowding hours of 11 to 3. The periods of observation never exceeded two hours, and usually lasted only 45 minutes to an hour. Each of the beach areas was observed both on warm sunny days when crowds were large and on cool foggy days when there were very few people at the beach. On a crowded day, there would be approximately 150 people in a given study area; on an uncrowded day about 35; and on an average day about 75. Since all three degrees of crowding were selected for each beach study area, the overall average was 75 people observed per hour. In 1976, the same three observers were joined by four additional observers. Following the same procedures in the same locations, 130 hours of observations were recorded on 70 separate days during July, August, and September. The 130 hours of observation were distributed equally among the same beach areas studied in 1975.

### The Frequency of Rule Violations

In 1975, when only 30 hours of observations were made, there were some differences in the frequency of rule violations, which varied from 1.5 per hour on South beach to over 3 per hour on County Beach. However, in 1976, when 130 hours of observation were conducted, there were no statistically significant differences at all between areas, with each averaging about one rule violation per hour (the highest frequency was 1.2 per hour, the least .9 per hour). Since the degree of crowding was controlled in the various areas, as was weather, and weekend or weekday crowds, it is unlikely that any of these factors affected the frequencies that were recorded. On the average, then, a population of approximately 75 beachgoers was observed to commit about one rule violation each hour. On crowded weekends this average is somewhat higher (about 1.6), and it falls below 1.0 on weekdays when the crowds are smaller. But we never observed more than four rule violations per hour under any conditions, and on several crowded days, no rule violations at all were seen during two hour-long periods of observation. In general, then, for a patch of sand roughly 35 by 50 yards containing some 75 people, the range of observable rule violations per hour is zero to four. We cannot be certain that additional days of observation would not yield slightly different frequencies, but the rate of rule violation observed was sufficiently constant that we believe it would alter only on special occasions or under special circumstances. Whether this rate of rule violation is interpreted as being high or low depends, of course, on the seriousness of the violations. An average of one murder or rape per hour would be intolerable for any set of beachgoers, while an average of one misdirected frisbee throw per hour would imply something altogether different.

### The Seriousness of Beach Rule Violations

It is difficult to estimate the seriousness of rule violations; one beachgoer may be outraged by frisbee throwing, but another may wink—literally—at a man who masturbates. Nevertheless, some differentiation of violations can be made.

For example, there are some violations that typically bother no one on the beach. Thus, drinking beer is a common violation that rarely bothers anyone, even the police. But there are other violations that do bother some people, such as the use of loud, obscene language, and the throwing of sand or balls. Finally, there are serious violations such as theft, assault, or indecent exposure that bother many beachgoers. In any case, the seriousness of a violation is most meaningfully determined by the reaction of the offended party.

Table 1 lists the relative frequency of violations separated into two categories: offenses that bothered a beachgoer, and those that did not. We see that 170 of the 192 total rule violations recorded in 1975 and 1976 led to no trouble of any kind; only 22 rule violations produced any sort of troubled reaction from an aggrieved party. To provide a better understanding of these rule violations and their apparent seriousness, it may prove useful to have a brief description of those that evoked no troubled reaction as well as those that did. Because there were no qualitative differences between violations seen in 1975 and 1976, only the violations seen in 1975 will be discussed here.

Fifty-two of the sixty-nine violations observed in 1975 pro-

**Table 1**

The Seriousness of Rule Violations on Southland
Beach in 1975–1976

|  | Area 15–16 | Area 8–11 | Area 24–27 | Area County | Total |
|---|---|---|---|---|---|
| Violations that did not produce a troubled reaction | 45 | 33 | 25 | 67 | 170 |
| Violations that did produce a troubled reaction | 11 | 5 | 4 | 2 | 22 |
| Percentage of troubled reactions | 20% | 13% | 14% | 3% | 11.4% |

duced no visible negative reaction. Twenty-eight of these violations involved dogs, drinking beer, or smoking marijuana. Although these are offenses against the municipal beach ordinances, rather than offenses against people, they do have some potential for evoking negative reaction from some beachgoers; however, in these 28 cases, no such reaction was seen. The following 26 rule violations had a somewhat greater potential for troubling other beachgoers, but once again, no negative reaction was observed.

1. A young woman with a male escort was hit by a frisbee; they both smiled wanly and the man threw it back without comment.

2. Two twelve-year-old boys undressed clumsily on the beach; one of the boys dropped his pants in the sand and stood naked for a few moments laughing embarrassedly. No one reacted.

3. A brother and sister, aged about six and seven, threw sand at one another, shouting angrily. No outsider was hit by the sand. The mother led the now tearful younger brother to the shower, saying loudly and for effect, "Having children is one of life's greatest experiences." No one responded.

4. A group of nine male and female Anglo teenagers talked and shouted loudly and obscenely, not only using four-letter words in abundance but mocking one another with threats of sexual conquest or physical combat. Adults all around them paid no apparent attention.

5. Three Chicano men, all fully dressed, plunked themselves down on the sand only four or five feet from four teenaged Anglo girls. The men stared openly and made sexually insinuating comments in Spanish; the girls did nothing to acknowledge the men's presence. When the men left, as they soon did, the girls laughed to themselves, but expressed no apparent alarm or indignation.

6. A teenaged couple began to pet heatedly despite the presence around them of several children and elderly people. No one appeared to object to this display of overt passion, and indeed, one man of about 50 seemed to enjoy the display.

7. A large Chicano family group moved onto the sparsely

settled beach, setting down their blankets and paraphernalia within a few feet of an Anglo family group; the Anglos neither moved nor gave any sign of displeasure.

8. Two large, athletic German-speaking men in their early thirties acrobatically kicked a soccer ball back and forth in a crowd of people along the wet sand near the water. Although the ball almost hit several people and the hurtling men almost trampled other people, no one gave any sign of annoyance.

9. A thin Anglo teenager sat down next to four Anglo teenaged girls whom he did not know before and asked for a match. After some initial nervousness and coolness by the girls, the one closest to him struck up a conversation and after about 30 minutes these two were engaged in obvious flirtation and even some very mild petting.

10. A teenaged Anglo girl played her radio so loudly that it was quite difficult to hear anything else within a distance of 15 yards or so. Although several people were within this range, no one moved away or said anything to her.

11. Four Anglo teenaged boys shouted obscenities back and forth despite the proximity of children and adult couples; no one moved away or spoke to the teenagers or appeared in any way to be distressed.

12. A small Spanish-speaking girl ran away from her family, refusing to return when called to in Spanish; an older woman of about 60 ran after her, shouting and kicking sand lightly on two couples. When the child was finally caught, she was spanked severely and dragged back crying through the sand to her family group. No one within sight reacted visibly to this sequence.

13. Two small boys kicked sand on several people as they ran by; no one reacted.

14. A teenaged girl near the water lost one breast out of her bikini top; a pre-teenaged girl nearby mentioned the occurrence to her mother, but both seemed amused rather than upset.

15. A fully but shabbily dressed man of 50 or so staggered along the sand apparently quite drunk; he veered away from

most people on the sand as he approached them, but he came quite close to several; no one moved, stared at him directly, or said anything to him.

16. Two young men who were engaged in horseplay in the shallow water threw wet sand at each other, accidentally hitting a young woman and her male escort as they passed by; no apology was given, and the couple moved on without comment or backward glance.

17. Two men in their twenties sat together talking when one reached into his own trunks as if to rearrange his genitals, then reached over to the other to squeeze first his thigh, then his genitals. The first man then walked over to a nearby young woman who returned with him to the second man, who seemed quite amused by the exchange. No one else appeared to pay any attention.

18. A teenager throwing a football to another boy almost hit a passing child of eight or so; there was no reaction by the child or anyone else.

19. A group of men in their twenties were playing catch with a football when an errant throw landed near a family group, spattering sand on them and their food. The ball was tossed back politely; no account was asked for and no apology was offered.

20. Two teenagers playing catch with a softball hit a sleeping man on the leg, waking him; he tossed the ball back to them without any visible annoyance.

21. A girl sitting alone on the beach was hit rather hard in the leg by a frisbee thrown by a man. She threw it back without a glance or comment; the man did not apologize.

22. A woman had both breasts fall out of her bikini while in shallow water up to her knees, and she made no effort to cover herself for almost a minute. A man noticed with apparent pleasure.

23. A young French-speaking man and two young French-speaking women wrestled in the sand for over five minutes; although the wrestling was violent, and one of the women momentarily exposed one breast, there was nothing

overtly sexual about the behavior. Several people watched the encounter, but with apparent pleasure rather than annoyance.

24. A woman who was talking to several other people near the waterline began to breast-feed her infant; there was no visible reaction on the part of others.

25. A white male of 20 or so kissed and hugged a black male of the same age while the two lay together on a towel. Although the kiss and hug were sexual, there was no further sexual play and no one in the area reacted visibly.

26. Three pre-teenage boys threw sand at each other, hitting an older woman and her child as they passed by. There was no noticeable reaction.

There are several points to be made about these 26 incidents. For one thing, the rules being violated were sometimes, as in the incidents involving sexual behavior, by no means clearly defined, or presumably universally agreed upon. Because we felt that this behavior violated what we had come to understand from beachgoers as commonly accepted rules of beach conduct, these episodes were counted as rule violations even though no one in the area seemed to object. It is also true, of course, that even where clear rules or beach ordinances are violated, people often do not react. This failure to take offense will be considered in a later chapter in some detail. Moreover, even though these 26 rule violations *could* have given offense leading to a complaint or argument, anyone would agree, we suppose, that the violations were not terribly serious. To be sure, some could have been troubling, as in the obscene menace of the teenagers' language and posturing, or a thrown football hitting a sleeping person, or a drunken man accosting a small child. But most were not really serious, even potentially. There was no assault, no rape, no theft, no serious injury. Instead, we found people throwing footballs, ogling girls or trying to pick them up, shouting obscene words, or playing a radio too noisily— nothing really to call a lifeguard or the police about. Let us consider, then, all of the rule violation incidents during the summers of 1975 and 1976—22 in all—that *did* lead to some kind of troubled reaction.

### Rule Violations That Led to Trouble

Only 22 of the 192 rule violations observed in 1975 and 1976, less than 11 percent of the total, can be said to have involved a manifestly negative response on the part of a beachgoer. What is more, in most of these 22 instances, the negative response was far from being serious. Several of the violations that led to a reaction were both ordinary beach problems and rather trivial in themselves. Two of these involved kicking sand. In both of these instances, young boys kicked sand on an adult man who responded with an angry look and a yell such as, "Hey, don't kick sand." Nothing further was said or done and the children neither slowed down their joyous gallop nor looked back to see what had happened. Two instances involved one group moving too close to another on the sand. One of these instances involving a Chicano family illustrates a common sort of occurrence in which a sizable party of beachgoers settles down quite near another party of people even though there is unoccupied sand all around. Sometimes nothing happens, but in this case, the party whom the newcomers moved next to looked visibly distressed, then abruptly picked up their belongings and moved some ten yards away. Nothing further took place. In the other similar instance, four Chicanos, both men and women, left their towels on the sand to swim. While they were in the water a group of Anglos arrived, and even though the beach was not overly crowded, these people placed their towels within two or three feet of those of the Chicanos. They also then left for a swim. When the four Chicanos returned, they looked startled and then angry to find that other people had placed towels virtually on top of their own. Muttering to themselves in annoyance, they moved their belongings some distance away.

In another minor incident, several teenaged Anglo boys were happily engaged in throwing beer cans into the surf, retrieving them, then repeating the sequence. The danger to swimmers and waders was obvious, but there was no obvious reaction from beachgoers until a lifeguard approached and ordered an end to the practice. In a final incident on County Beach, a dishevelled "bum" who is a "regular" at this beach panhandled a young man, who swore at him in anger and ordered him away, threatening him with a "punch in the face" if he were seen on the beach again.

A somewhat more troublesome set of violations had to do with sexual encounters. Eleven such encounters were observed which drew a troubled reaction from an offended person. For example, in one encounter, two quite attractive blond teenaged girls were lying on their backs quietly talking to one another. Two teenaged boys who were returning to their towels from a refreshment stand saw the girls and altered their course in order to walk by them. Approaching to within two feet they slowed almost to a halt and one of the boys said quite loudly, "Want a beer?" and then without waiting for a response added "Want to fuck?" The girl closest to them did not even bother to stop her own conversation as she casually raised her hand toward them and then insultingly elevated her middle finger. The two boys left hurriedly without another word, looking thoroughly squelched.

In another incident, a young Swedish-speaking couple walked onto the beach fully clothed. They sat close to the berm and the man quickly pulled off his clothes down to a pair of very small bikini briefs, then walked to the water. The young woman then began a ritual of changing clothes which is common in Europe, but rarely seen on Southland Beach. First she took out of her purse a black bikini top which she tied around her waist. Pushing the bikini under her white T-shirt, she fastened it in place and removed the shirt. By now, several people—men and women alike—were watching. She then stood up and tied a very small white towel around her waist. Balancing delicately, she tried to wriggle out of her jeans without losing the towel. She managed to remove her jeans while affording no more than occasional glimpses of her now naked posterior, but when she tried to pull on her bikini bottoms, the towel fell altogether, and she stood nude for a long moment while she tried to catch the towel and pull on her bottoms, failing to do either. She finally abandoned the towel and simply pulled on her bikini, but by this time people were staring in frank amazement. Although the watching men hardly seemed to be offended by the spectacle, some women clearly were not pleased. One was heard to say with disgust, "That was really gross. Who does she think she is?" And another said to her female companion, "If you think that was bad, stick around for the next act; there's no telling what she'll do next." The first woman and her older female companion soon thereafter left the beach. Whether they did so as a result of the incident is not known.

In a third incident, an Anglo couple in their fifties lay on towels together on a crowded patch of sand. Both were quite pale, and from their clothing piled next to them, they could have been tourists. After some minutes of talking to one another they began to kiss and pet, quite avidly. Everyone in the area looked on startled; teenagers sometimes neck at the beach, but people in their fifties do so rarely, if ever. As the necking continued and became more intimate, several people looked embarrassed and one woman about 35 took her ten-year-old daughter by the hand and abruptly left the beach. Others may have wanted to do so, because one could feel the embarrassment in the air, and several beachgoers could be overheard discussing this couple's behavior in disapproving terms.

As we will learn when we discuss our interviews with beachgoers, quite a few women are offended by the necking that sometimes takes place on the beach. In four instances that we observed, teenaged necking evoked considerable displeasure from older people nearby. The most common response to necking on the beach is for other people to look momentarily startled, then look away as if embarrassed. Sometimes a solitary man, frequently hidden behind sunglasses, stares with voyeuristic pleasure. One seldom observes obvious indications that people are upset by what is going on, but people *were* upset by the following episodes.

First, at County Beach, a pretty teenaged girl began to neck with one of her two male companions. After ten minutes of moderately zealous necking, the male got up and left, presumably to go into the water farther down the beach. As soon as he left, the other boy began to neck with the girl and their passion was well beyond that usually seen on the beach. He put his hands under her bikini top and inside her cut-off jeans. She caressed his genitals, and they alternated in lying atop one another while making copulatory motions. Two nearby couples were embarrassed to the point of obvious anger by this display. No one said anything that could be overheard, but one couple quickly left the area, glancing back in what appeared to be disgust.

A similar sexual display was presented by a blond girl in a see-through bikini and her teenaged boyfriend. What appeared to be a family grouping of a mother, grandmother, and two small children first attempted to ignore the sexual behavior, then picked up their belongings and moved about 100 yards away. A nearby teenaged couple ignored the necking for about 15 minutes, then they too picked up their gear and moved, this time about 50 yards away. In two similar episodes, passionate sexual embraces on the beach led nearby beachgoers to express their annoyance verbally, then to move away.

Two other troubling incidents involved fully clothed, elderly voyeurs who meandered along the beach ogling young women. On two occasions such men came so close to a woman and stared so openly that the woman reacted with obvious annoyance, grimacing, and turning away. One appeared to say something that could not be overhead. When the voyeurs finally left, both of these women stared after them with murderous looks.

Another cause of troubled reactions was attempted "pickups." On one such occasion two young black men in street clothes approached a young blond woman who was alone on the sand. After many suggestive remarks they asked her to go with them "for a drink." She ignored them. When she continued to ignore their increasingly suggestive comments and questions, one of the men bristled and angrily called her a "honky bitch." After that, the men walked away. As soon as they did so, the woman grabbed her possessions and moved away in the opposite direction. In another episode, two attractive blond girls about 16 years old had just arrived on the beach and were lying on their stomachs with their bikini tops fastened. They had done nothing provocative when a quite handsome man of 35 or so, who happened to be a volleyball player and a "regular" at this part of the beach, walked by. He paused, then flopped down on the sand behind the girls. As if he knew them, he reached out and grabbed one girl by her ankle. She was clearly startled, even angry, and pulled her leg away; she refused to turn over to look at the man or talk to him. Her girlfriend, whom he had not grabbed, did roll over. Hesitantly and with a look of profound awkwardness, she modestly exchanged words with him for about five minutes while he continued to lie on his stomach in the sand. He renewed his attempts to talk to the first girl, but she ignored him, quite insultingly. After five minutes, he left and the girls discussed his "pick-up" attempt with obvious annoyance, gesturing in a ridiculing manner. Among snatches of their conversation that were audible the girl who had been touched said that it was very "uncool" for a man to "come on to them" that way.

In these sexually tinged episodes, some people were annoyed, perhaps even quite upset, but the resulting "trouble," if it can properly be called that, was slight. In five other episodes, physical harm was threatened, and more fearful or angry reactions were evoked. Two of these instances had to do with roughhouse games in the shallow water. It is commonplace for young men to play roughly in the water, throwing footballs, wrestling, or running at top speed despite the presence of women, children, and elderly people all around. As we have seen, usually no one complains, but in two instances that were observed, people were clearly alarmed. In the first, four Chicano men, all fully clothed, took turns carrying one another into the water, then dumping the victim and running away. The victim pursued his tormentors heedless of people around him. It was all good fun, but recklessly done, and people in the water quickly moved aside, giving the men ample room for their frolic, and evincing fear and anger as they did so. As some of the displaced bathers returned to the sand, one man was heard to say, "You'd think they owned the beach," and another woman said "Why doesn't the lifeguard do something? They could really hurt somebody running around like that."

In the second instance, five Anglo men in their early twenties were playing a game of football in the shallow water despite the fact that the water was already occupied by children and women who were quietly wading and splashing in the water. The men threw the football hard and when the ball went astray, as it often did, it became a dangerous projectile, especially where small children were concerned. They also ran at top speed, mindless of the people around them. People moved away to give them room, but one woman who was in the water with her small child said something angrily to one of them, and glared with obvious displeasure at a man who ran by almost hitting her. She then took her child and left the water glaring back angrily as she did. The young man continued the game for only a minute or two after that and then returned to the sand, apparently chastened by the woman's rebuke. In both of these instances a lifeguard was close at hand but he did nothing and no one complained to him. In a third instance a man playing catch with a frisbee hit a girl who was lying on the sand with another young woman. She did not appear to be painfully hurt, but she did glare at the man and then spoke to him in clear annoyance. He apologized with apparent concern and moved away to continue his game elsewhere.

In a fourth encounter, several teenaged Anglos were playing a rather listless game of catch with a football when two ten-year-old boys, who were fully dressed, passed by them as they left the beach for the day. Without warning, a large teenager unleashed a Tarzan yell and roughly tackled one of the smaller boys, rolling him in the sand and knocking his possessions out of his hands. The small victim of the surprise tackle was clearly frightened, and while he was helped up with a sort of apologetic grin, he was near tears and yelled, unoriginally but sincerely, "Leave me alone, you big bully." The "bully" looked somewhat abashed, as did his friends, and as the smaller boy walked quickly away, brushing sand off his clothes, the bully said plaintively, "People who feel like that shouldn't come to the beach." None of the other teenagers said anything to confirm this opinion, however, and it was apparent that they shared the smaller boy's view that the surprise tackle was uncalled for.

A final incident serves particularly well to illustrate what appears to be the typical response of beachgoers to behavior that suggests physical menace. At a spot about 10 yards from a lifeguard tower and only a few yards from the observer's towel, two 15- or 16-year-old Anglo boys who were walking along the beach stopped and began to yell at each other. Both wore jeans but no shirts, and each appeared to have been drinking, one staggeringly so. Their conversation, which was already loud, quickly led to a shouting match with one boy— the less drunk of the two—teasing the other and playfully pushing him. The drunker of the boys took great offense, saying "Man, I'm serious, man, don't do that or I'll kill you," and similar things. All the while he was clenching his fists and raising them as if to strike, while the other boy continued to giggle and push him teasingly. After a few minutes of this sparring, the drunker of the two ran to the water, doused himself thoroughly, then wet and shivering he ran back, kicking sand all over the observer and others nearby, none of whom reacted. When he returned, the argument continued—obscene shouts were exchanged, both boys balled their fists, and an actual fight appeared to be imminent. Two nearby couples quickly grabbed their towels and moved away, but just at the point where serious blows seemed to be inevitable, the two boys walked off parallel to the water, stopping every ten yards or so to square off, to threaten mayhem, and to exchange loud obscene insults. As they moved along, people on the crowded beach parted like the Red Sea, grabbing their possessions and children, and retreating out of the boys' path to a safe distance. It was not only women and children who scuttled away; young men did so as well. Neither of the combatants was particularly large or well-muscled, yet groups of larger and stronger men moved away from them. No one attempted to intervene in the dispute, and no one spoke directly to them about their obscene language, their scuffling which kicked sand onto people, or their threatened combat. People simply moved out of their path and the boys eventually staggered out of the area. After their departure, the beach buzzed with critical and annoyed comments as people returned their towels to the places they had just vacated. Almost everyone seemed quite disturbed, but no one had done anything to confront the boys directly, nor did anyone complain to the nearby lifeguard.

This pattern of avoiding confrontations is characteristic of the beach. Most potentially troublesome rule violations evoke no response whatsoever. For the most part, people appear to ignore behavior altogether. As a police officer said, they seem to "tune out" one another. When a rule violation does provoke some reaction, the most common one is for the offended party simply to move some distance away. Words are not usually exchanged and accounts are seldom demanded, but when a complaint is uttered, or a "dirty look" is given, that seems to be as far as the offended person cares to go, since the next step tends to be away from confrontation and almost always involves an increased physical separation between the parties involved. We will discuss this pattern of avoiding conflict in more detail later, after more evidence has been presented.

### Conclusion

Up and down Southland Beach during the summers of 1975 and 1976, rule violations seldom occurred, and when they did they were for the most part inconsequential insofar as the well-being of beachgoers was concerned. Almost half of all rule violations that were seen involved beer, marijuana, or dogs, and although such offenses could conceivably have led to interpersonal conflict, these did not. Indeed, more than half of the violations that had a potential for interpersonal conflict produced no reaction from beachgoers. When a reaction did occur, it usually seemed calculated to avoid further trouble, not to make an issue of the trouble that had already been experienced.

As we knew from the police, from lifeguards, and from our ethnographic observations here and there on the beach, serious trouble can indeed occur, and beachgoers sometimes do confront one another with anger and sometimes with violence. However, in 192 hours of systematic observation—during which all rule violations, even the most trivial, and beachgoers' reactions to them, were recorded—we saw little trouble, and none that we saw was really serious. We saw no serious injuries on the sand or in the water, no theft, no assaults, no men exposing themselves, no children being molested sexually. No one complained to a lifeguard, and no one called the police. Furthermore, the supposedly troublesome areas just south and north of the pier were not very different from the other parts of the beach. Rules were violated no more often in these areas than anywhere else, and even though there was a somewhat greater likelihood that a rule violation in these areas would lead to a troubled reaction (see Table 1), the trouble was a long way from being serious. It seems reasonable to conclude that during peak crowding hours (10 A.M. to 4 P.M.) in the summer, the trouble that beachgoers experience on the sandy beach is both relatively infrequent and inconsequential.

# 6

## Trouble at the Beach: Strange and Menacing People

The findings of Chapter Five suggest that rule violations on any given part of the sandy beach itself are so infrequent and so minor that a beachgoer can ordinarily look forward to a day at Southland Beach with little concern that anything troublesome will occur. But there is another source of potential trouble or unease at Southland Beach that we have not yet explored. That source is the presence of "strange" people whose appearance may be upsetting even though their actual behavior violates no law or rule. Such persons are common on and around Southland Beach, and they may play an important part in determining whether beachgoers think of the beach as a safe or dangerous place. Not all trouble on the beach occurs on the sand, as we learned from lifeguards and police officers. The beach is bordered by parking lots, refreshment stands, bathrooms, and walkways, and it is in these "fringe" areas of the beach that deviant-appearing people are most common. Their presence in these places could disturb an otherwise relaxed beachgoer.[1]

Not even the local Chamber of Commerce would try to suggest that everyone who goes to the beach is either a tanned blond girl in a skimpy bikini or an athletic young man with a surfboard. There are some beautiful specimens, to be sure, but most beachgoers are quite ordinary in appearance, a good many are decidedly unattractive, and some are clearly obese or physically handicapped. And among this most diverse assemblage of people there are some whose appearance is so strange or unusual that they may frighten, embarrass or offend others.

Many of the people we met and interviewed at Southland Beach mentioned such people, calling them "weirdos," "bums," "perverts," "mentals," "psychos," "weird Harolds," and the like. Some said that these people disturbed them, and others said they avoided parts of the beach where they felt they might encounter people of this kind. For example, 27 of the 66 women who were interviewed on the beach said that they had been upset or bothered by someone's appearance at the beach. Although it was difficult to determine the extent to which these beachgoers were bothered by someone's appearance, it seems quite likely that beachgoers' experience of the beach as safe or dangerous, pleasant or uncomfortable, is influenced strongly by the kind of people they see there. Thus, beachgoers often say that they dislike and avoid areas where the people are not "nice," like them, but are instead dirty, drunken, perverted, weird, or otherwise bothersome. As one woman beachgoer on North beach put it: "I like this part of the beach because everyone here is so nice. I never go down around the pier anymore. Some of the people there are really creepy. I just don't feel comfortable there."

Police officers and lifeguards confirm that some of the people at Southland Beach are very strange indeed, and receive their official attention as suspicious persons. For example, lifeguards may be called upon to investigate a report that a strange-looking man is kissing women's bellies as he walks up and down the beach, or the police may investigate a woman's complaint that she was lifted into the air by a "weird looking" man who immediately threw her back down on the sand and left without saying a word. In such cases, however, it is what these people did, not simply how they looked, that caused the concern. Some people at the beach are exceed-

Unusual sand sculpture; a shark and a woman.

ingly strange in appearance, yet they never behave in any manner that calls for action to be taken against them.* Thus the lifeguards recognize many "regular weirds" but insist that they are harmless. Some may be labeled "lookers"—men who look at women from a discreet distance—and regarded as harmless. Others who actually approach and talk to women—"hummers"—may be thought of as being more troublesome. So it is with "pier creeps," "hermits," and "mentals"—many are known and tolerated because despite their appearance they break no laws and do not cause beachgoers to make formal complaints about them. A kind of

*It must be acknowledged that appearances probably never stand alone, because they almost certainly evoke expectations of certain kinds of behavior. It must also be noted that much of what is reported here mixes appearances with behaviors. The point, nevertheless, is that unlike rule violations as such, the people noted in this chapter for the most part broke no explicable rule.

legendary figure is one "Sandy Andy," who startled women on Southland Beach in the 1940s by wetting himself in the water, then rolling about on the beach until he was covered with sand from head to foot. He would then sit close to some unsuspecting woman and stare at her. Some women must have been alarmed by this whimsical approach, but Sandy Andy was known to the lifeguards as a harmless character, not a menace.

The question for us is how many and what kinds of deviant-appearing people there are at the beach, and how beachgoers react to their presence. We shall describe and analyze what we saw concerning such anomalous people during two summers of systematic beach observation, but first some background information should be presented concerning the fringes of the beach and the sandy beach itself.

### The Beach Fringe

Beachgoers often complain about the strange or bothersome people they see as they approach the beach, park their car, go to a public bathroom, or buy refreshments. Some of these complaints have to do with conduct such as that exhibited—literally—by a man who stood up suddenly from behind a shrub to reveal that he had dropped his pants to his ankles. But many complaints have to do solely with appearances: a shabbily dressed man sitting near a parking lot; a pair of "tough" young men near a refreshment stand; a woman in the bathroom whose face twitched.

During the course of this research, we often saw people whose appearance was potentially disturbing in the various fringe areas of the beach. For example, there was a shabbily dressed American Indian man, who leaned against a parking meter and stared at women who passed by, and an unbelievably ragged old man who walked through the parking lot looking vaguely furtive. A derelict, perhaps somewhat drunk and certainly filthy, walked by the entrance to the women's bathroom, and a "bum" sat outside the door to another women's bathroom, perhaps watching women enter and leave, perhaps not. Three tattooed Chicano teenagers seemed

Man on the fringe of the beach.

menacing as they sauntered back and forth in front of a hot dog stand, but they broke no rules. All they actually did was walk and posture. A ragged man with a burlap sack on his shoulder pawed through a trash can looking for bottles, all the while talking to himself in a loud but incoherent mumble. An elderly man tottered, perhaps drunkenly, along the walkway dressed in a rumpled black suit complete with black bow tie. Another man, this one younger but also possibly drunk, was showering at one of the many public showers set back on the sand toward the parking lots—he was naked and when a passing woman saw him, he attempted to put on a pair of trousers only to trip and fall down in the sand. Whether in terms of appearances alone or appearances plus behavior, all of these people were likely to be memorable for anyone who saw them, but whether they would be seen as alarming or merely curious would obviously vary from viewer to viewer.

It was difficult to make prolonged systematic observations in some of the fringe areas. An observer in these areas was sometimes conspicuous so that some strange people tended to veer away, suspecting, no doubt, an undercover police officer. Only in one fringe setting, the promenade, was it possible to observe carefully for any length of time without having any perceptible effect on the people in that area. These observations will be presented later in this chapter.

### Strange People on the Beach Itself

Strange and menacing people are not confined to fringe areas of the beach. Beachgoers also tell of strange folk such as Sandy Andy whom they have seen on the sandy beach. One beachgoer told of seeing a man walking along the sand on one of the year's hottest days wearing a fur coat and fur hat. Another saw a stroller who was totally nude. Many reported shabbily dressed men who walked along the sand, often pausing to stare at someone. Others said that they were once startled to see someone on the beach who was apparently psychotic or mentally ill, and one person complained about a blind man who walked along the beach tapping ahead of himself with a cane and stepping over, not around, recumbent bodies when he encountered them.

In our hundreds of hours spent on the beach we also saw many persons whose appearance was decidedly unusual. Two mentally retarded men—both with bicycles whose horns they often honked—were regularly seen on the sand. One usually stopped to look at pretty girls and to honk his horn. We found both men to be totally inoffensive, as did the lifeguards, but some women we spoke to found them annoying, and a few were frightened. Other women knew one of these men well and always spoke to him warmly. We also saw a variety of people who carried large transistor radios which they listened to through earphones—one such man, a black man dressed in green satin, danced as he ran along; another man, white this time, also danced as he walked along, alternating slow sinuous movements with ballet-like leaps. We twice saw young female baton twirlers at the water's edge.

One day two men were noticed sitting together under a
large beach umbrella near tower 4 on North beach; one was
very old, the other was of an age to be his son. Each sat
formally on a wooden chair, each was dressed in a dark suit
and the older man also wore a scarf and a hat. They sat
together without speaking for hours. Another man in his forties, dressed in a shirt and short pants, walked along North
beach chewing alternately on a plastic bag or a folded news-
paper; from time to time he stopped to converse with someone, which he did more or less rationally, although he stood
well beyond normal speaking distance, then left them with
his card identifying him as an "electronic jack-of-all-trades."
As he left, he began chewing once again.

We saw two men dressed in complete Santa Claus suits
carrying a sign that, upon closer inspection, was advertising a
movie. We also saw three women in bathing suits sitting and
lying on the sand at tower 16. They spoke what sounded like
Hungarian, but what was most remarkable about them was
their size. The smallest must have weighed 300 pounds and
the largest could have weighed 400 pounds. Beachgoers
stared at them in awe.

Sometimes strange people are seen in the water. One elderly man was seen to go swimming while fully dressed and
wearing a beret. Two fully dressed young people rode their
bicycles in the shallow water then waded, still fully dressed,
out into the sea. No one paid them any apparent attention.
On another occasion a strange-looking man walked down the
beach, sat under a lifeguard tower, and removed his sweater
and tennis shoes. Wearing levis, a shirt, and one sock, he
walked into the water and swam farther and farther out to
sea. Several beachgoers watched as he swam happily, spout-
ing water like a whale. A lifeguard watched with apparent
unconcern for several minutes, then a lifeguard jeep arrived
and two guards swam out to bring him back in. He came in
without complaint and answered the lifeguard's questions
politely, but he rolled his eyes in a strange way and spoke
rather mystically about the Colorado River. The lifeguards
thought he was on drugs; what the beachgoers who watched
all this thought is not known.

While strange people like these are commonplace at Southland Beach, they are not necessarily everyday sights on all
parts of the beach. To understand how common such people
are and how ordinary beachgoers respond to them, let us
consider again the beach areas that were reported upon in
Chapter Five. You will recall that various areas of the beach
were systematically observed. In addition to recording all rule
violations and beachgoers' reactions to them, we recorded all
conspicuously curious or strange people, even though they
violated no rule, and we also noted how beachgoers responded to the presence of these people. In terms of rule
violations as such, it was found that neither area 16 just south
of the pier, nor area 15 just north of it, was distinctive in the
amount or kind of rule violation seen. But when these same
areas were looked at again in terms of the deviant-appearing
people seen there, they were indeed distinctive: they had
substantially greater numbers of strange or menacing people
than any other portion of the beach.

Thus at County Beach, the only deviant-appearing people
commonly seen were gay men, and they are such a natural
part of the beach environment in that area that beachgoers
rarely pay them any attention. Only one other deviant appearing person was seen at all—this was a ragged alcoholic
man who regularly slept on a bench that ironically read "support your local police." He frequently panhandled from
County Beach regulars, who rarely expressed annoyance.
Moving to the next area of observation around towers 8 and
9, only two questionable persons were seen. One was a man
wearing green jockey shorts instead of bathing trunks. Given
the common use of European-styled bikini bathing suits,
jockey shorts are not that odd, and most people on the beach
probably paid this man no attention. The other unusual person seen was one of the previously mentioned mentally retarded men with a bicycle who often passed through honking
at girls.

At the extreme southern end of the beach (towers 24–27),
three strange-appearing people were seen. One was the same
retarded man with bike and horn. A second was an Anglo
man of 45 or so, wearing a T-shirt, baggy pants, and tennis

A man looks at women.

shoes, whose closely crewcut hair was almost as distinctive as the amount of camera equipment he carried. He had several cameras, a set of lens and filters, a tripod and a large tele-photo lens. He seemed to be more interested in women than in the seascape. Beachgoers looked at him askance, but none seemed unduly upset. The final person was a man of 50 or so, asleep in the sand. He was barefooted but wore ragged pants, an old plaid shirt, black suspenders, and a stocking cap. He had wrapped a jacket around his head. Every so often he rolled over in the sand and after two hours of sleep on a hot afternoon he arose and shakily shambled off. People avoided him as he lay on the sand and they moved out of his path as he left.

In 17 hours of careful observation at these three areas, only these six persons were recorded as being exceptionally noteworthy in appearance. At areas 15 and 16, however, 13 hours of observation produced 16 people or sets of people whose appearance was strange or menacing. Let us briefly consider these people and the reactions of ordinary beachgoers to them.

In area 16, on a warm sunny day, a young blond man ran along the beach dressed as a prizefighter in training might be. He wore heavy boots, green rugby stockings, red nylon knickers, and a red nylon jacket with a towel around his neck. As he ran along the waterline, he stopped every so often, and despite the presence of a large number of bathers, strollers, and fellow runners, he began to shadow box, punching savagely at an invisible opponent, all the while grunting and snorting with exertion. He continued this exhibition for some ten minutes before turning away from the water and leaving by tramping back through the soft sand. Hundreds of people saw him, but as he approached them all quickly looked away and maintained an apparently purposeful and disciplined lack of attention. People acted as if they feared that any attention given the man might cause him to launch blows at real targets.

A fair-skinned young woman wearing a loose fitting grey sweatshirt with a silk scarf tied around her waist, baggy black pants, and green hightop tennis shoes walked across the sand toward the water. Her head was shaved bald. She walked with a muscular black man who was wearing a Mickey Mouse T-shirt and green bathing trunks. As the girl (who was apparently an initiate of a nearby drug treatment center whose members shave their heads as they begin therapy) sat in the shallow water, she bent forward to touch her forehead to the wavelets. The man ignored her. After about five minutes, she rose, shook the water out of her pants, and walked away. As she walked she chanted something unintelligible to the observer. The man walked slowly after her. No one on the beach appeared to pay her or the man even the slightest attention.

Toward the rear of the beach lay a portly man of 50 or so, asleep in the hot sand. He wore only bathing trunks and as he slept in the blazing sun, he sweated. Every so often he would wake and roll over. After several such rolls he was as covered with sand as Sandy Andy. As people passed him on their way to or from the beach, they invariably looked startled; surely he resembled nothing that was commonly seen on the beach. Two people were heard to ask their companions if they thought he was dead. No one stopped to investigate, but mothers took their small children by the hand and steered them away. Yet no one called a lifeguard or the police, and after an hour and a half he arose and like a sandy apparition walked off the beach and up a nearby street, without either showering or brushing off the sand. People who met him in transit looked startled and seemed to pass him at a greater distance than would be usual.

Three young men walked along the waterline. All wore costumes that were bizarre enough to startle the most flamboyant rock star. One carried a guitar in a case that was painted to resemble an American flag. One played a flute and the third sang rather loudly while doing dance steps in the sand. They gave a brief impromptu concert for a minute or two, then seriously, even rather glumly, walked back through the sand away from the beach. Only a handful of beachgoers appeared to notice, and these only glanced up briefly and then turned away. Their apparent disinterest was difficult to fathom, since the strangely costumed men and their music were conspicuous, even bizarre, and few musicians of any sort stroll along this beach.

Two black teenagers walked—or swaggered—their way across the sand, looking at women as they went. They swaggered in the characteristic manner of street gang members, and their expressions were studiously contemptuous or menacing. They were obviously determined to look "tough." Each wore black pointed shoes, tight trousers, and a fishnet undershirt. Each also had his hair done up in bright pink curlers, over which was worn a green hairnet. As the boys passed by, several people turned to watch them, although no one looked until the boys' backs were turned, and all avoided eye contact. A nearby middle-class appearing black woman said to another black woman in an exasperated tone, "Oh, my God. What next?"

A 50-year-old man, wearing an Aloha shirt, bermuda shorts, white socks and street shoes, was observed meandering across the sand with an enormous pair of binoculars fixed to his eyes. His odyssey was made stranger still by the fact that he was stooped forward at almost a 45-degree angle. So extreme was his forward tilt that when he peered into his binoculars it was difficult to understand how he could see anything but the sand at his feet, yet he marched onward and looked through his binoculars. On closer inspection it became obvious that his odd posture served a purpose, since he did indeed locate the targets of his inquiry very close to his feet. For example, he almost literally stood over a voluptuous young woman and stared at her through his glasses. After a few moments, he moved on to the next attractive woman and repeated his inspection. He was observed doing this for 40 minutes, yet at no time did any beachgoer display marked concern about his activities. A few men noticed him and smiled, but then went back to whatever they were doing. Various women obviously saw what he was up to, but they all avoided giving any clear sign that they knew he existed. One of the lifeguards commented that the man, who was known as Mr. Peepers, was a harmless and regular visitor to this part of the beach.

On the same day that Mr. Peepers was closely examining the pulchritude on the beach, one woman became the cynosure of all eyes. This woman was in her mid- to late twenties. She wore one of the tiniest string bikinis ever manufactured. What was remarkable about this was the fact that she was a very short person who weighed at least 250 pounds. After lying in the sun all by herself, she arose to go for refreshments and as she did so, virtually everyone within sight—as if by prearranged signal—rose slightly from their towels and stared at her. She walked with a studied wiggle and the bikini strings covered very few of the moving parts. People not only stared at her, they continued to stare until she vanished from sight, then they turned to their companions and discussed what they had just seen. Many beachgoers say that they are intrigued or repelled by obese people on the beach; this

View toward area 15.

episode demonstrates vividly that an obese person, especially one in an almost nonexistent bathing suit, can indeed become the focus of attention for almost everyone.

At area 15, just north of the pier, nine comparable sights were seen. In the least remarkable of these, a man of perhaps 80 years was seen tottering along the waterline. He was notable not only for his advanced age, but for the fact that he was wearing a straw boater, a white shirt and tie, and a seersucker jacket over a pair of old-fashioned, almost knee-length bathing trunks. On his feet were tennis shoes. He carried a cane but this was merely brandished at nearby seagulls and waders as he passed by. He had a set expression that suggested mayhem if crossed, and people were quick to give him and his walking stick room. They moved out of his path as he approached, and then gazed after him in wonderment rather than fear.

Next was a camera buff who set up his 35mm telephoto-lens-equipped camera on a tripod close to the waterline. He wore a regular business suit distinguished only by the fact that it was badly frayed. He removed his shoes, which he hung from a corner of the tripod. Whenever a fetching young woman came into sight, he bowed formally, took off his golf cap, and motioned for her to pose. Most obliged and he snapped a picture. If they declined and walked away as some did, he once or twice moved his tripod and snapped them from the rear. Despite the unusual appearance of this man and his singular photographic enterprise, none of the nearby beachgoers paid him more than passing attention. After 30 minutes or so he left and no one stared after him as he did so.

Somewhat later on the same day, a wizened, deeply tanned man of 60 or more years made his way across the sand toward a mass of beachgoers who were collected around the berm. He wore a battered straw hat, a cotton shirt and pants, and was barefooted. He had a one-foot square piece of cardboard in one hand, and a package in Christmas wrapping in the other. As he walked by he was audibly talking to himself, and several people on the beach—young and old alike—turned to watch him as he passed by. Some seemed concerned about where he would locate himself, but when he moved on, they relaxed. He finally settled down and proceeded to strip down to a pair of modern swimming trunks; he then sat on the piece of cardboard and opened the Christmas package which proved to hold his lunch, a racy novel, and a book of cross-word puzzles. He spent over an hour enjoying the sun, his lunch, and the book, and gave every indication of being a slightly odd beach regular, not at all someone to be concerned about. No one paid him any lasting notice.

At about the same time, a strange figure appeared at the waterline. He was a man of 65 or so, very large, but not fat, dressed in a pair of farmer's overalls and nothing else. He was entirely bald and as he walked, he weaved from side to side lurching first into the water, then back out toward people sitting or lying on the berm overlooking it. At first he appeared to be drunk and people withdrew from him. One woman went to collect her small daughter and get her out of his path. It soon became apparent, however, that the man's problem was neurological—his gait was unsteady but regular, like an exaggerated case of cerebral palsy, and he bore straight ahead if one allowed for the zig-zag deviations he made. As people appeared to realize that he was not drunk they seemed to relax somewhat, but they still watched him until he passed by them and until it was clear that he was moving on, not staying there to cause them any trouble.

On another day, a crowded weekend, a modishly dressed fully clothed man walked across the sand escorting a beautiful young woman in a white bikini. They went directly to the waterline where he directed her in a variety of poses while he took photographs of her—lying in the sand, frolicking in the water, wading up to her waist, doing exercises, running and the like. A few beachgoers watched, perhaps attracted by the girl's beauty, perhaps by the man's photography. Some teenage males even stopped to stare, grinning broadly as they admired the woman. After a while, the photographer moved back on the sand, where he posed her again and took more pictures. Finally they stopped. He abruptly left, going to his car in the lot and driving away. She returned to the water and swam very competently. At this point the onlookers really sat up. What *was* going on? Was she a hired model? Would he be back? People looked and talked and waited. He did not return and the girl walked down the waterline and away after finishing her swim, leaving everyone baffled about the relationship between the photographer and the woman. No danger here, but an obvious puzzle.

Along the same waterline two distinctive young men made their way. They wore trousers, but were naked to the waist. They were strongly muscled and heavily tattooed, although they were too old and too long-haired to be servicemen. They looked instead like gangsters, perhaps Mafiosi, and they exuded menace. Beachgoers quite dramatically gave them a wide berth. Without any outward show of alarm, everyone who was in their path moved back on the sand, or further into the water, and people who were walking toward them changed course so as not to pass by too closely. No one stared after them, although a few glanced, perhaps fearing to be caught doing so. Fear was the common reaction, and it was obvious.

Soon thereafter another striking pair strolled the waterline: a man of about 50 and a woman about 40. The man was blond with his hair shaved to about three inches above his ears. He walked clumsily, like Frankenstein, with his arms and legs stiffly held out in front, and his facial expression was startlingly blank. His appearance was not normalized by the fact that he wore purple trousers rolled up to the knees, no shirt at all, and red suspenders. He had large, red, ulcerated sores all over his back and lower legs. The woman was black and very busty. She wore a shimmery silver evening dress, but no shoes. She also wore a bright, carroty orange wig which made her appearance comic because the wind continually rearranged it on her head. The two of them—one lurching, the other walking normally—slowly made their way along the waterline. The same people who had appeared to be so nervous in the presence of the tattooed men, gave these people almost no attention at all. They were indifferent.

On a third day, people did attend noticeably to the antics of an incredibly athletic Asian man who performed kung fu-like exercises on the sand. He was young, lithe, and handsome, hardly a menacing or strange figure, but when he began his exercise routine he whirled, gestured, thrusted, kicked, snorted, shouted, roared, and finally screamed. People stared and stared some more. He did not invite close attention. Instead he seemed to radiate stay-away signals, and no one approached him or clustered around. People watched him, but they did so from a respectable distance. After twenty minutes, when he left, people visibly relaxed.

On this same day a noteworthy group was observed. A blond man with several tattoos on his arms and chest was smilingly escorting four women—three white and one black. The women all wore blond wigs, were heavily made-up, and looked, frankly, "cheap." It took the observer about 30 seconds to conclude that this party must consist of a pimp and his four prostitutes. It took even less time to determine that literally everyone on the beach within 100 feet or so was staring with a kind of open fascination otherwise seen on the beach only in the presence of the previously mentioned fat lady in the string bikini. The man and the four women talked, briefly played cards, and one woman waded. All four women massaged the man's neck and back at one point, and he in turn massaged each of their backs with suntan lotion. After about 45 minutes, they left together, walking to a new white Cadillac in the parking lot. Beachgoers watched them go with rapt attention. So frank was this inspection, and so uncharacteristic, that the observer asked two nearby persons what they made of these five beachgoers. Both of them—a teenaged boy of 16 or so, and a woman of 35 to 40—agreed that they were watching four "hookers" and their "manager" on their day off. The young man speculated that since four out of five of the strange party were very pale, they could not be accustomed to the beach—which was, in his opinion, a good thing, since he said, "There's no telling what diseases they could leave behind in the sand."

### The South Beach Promenade

It would appear that strange or frightening people are present more often just north and south of the pier than they are anywhere else on the beach. What is more, for beachgoers to reach area 16, and to a somewhat lesser extent area 15, they must cross the promenade, a place which seems to attract a remarkable number of strange and wondrous people. Let us look at this hodgepodge of humanity and then examine how beachgoers behave when they encounter these people on the walkway.

As we mentioned in Chapter Two, the promenade is a fifteen- to twenty-foot wide strip of concrete bordered by sand, volleyball courts, and a grassy gymnastics area on one side and by refreshment stands, shops, parking lots, and run-down apartments on the other. People of all sorts, most of them fully dressed, stroll along this walkway stopping now and then to watch the gymnastics or to ogle women beachgoers, or just to eat and rest. Many ride bicycles, darting in and out of the strollers, somehow avoiding the collisions that would appear to be inevitable. Now and then a police officer riding a three-wheel motorcycle slowly cruises up and down. Many of these strollers live or work in the area; some are transients dressed in rags; some are wealthy tourists, often from foreign countries. A few are elegantly dressed men and women who appear to have come to the beach from Beverly Hills for a day of slumming. One hears a veritable babel of languages—not only Spanish, which is common, but French, German, Swedish, Hungarian, Russian, Polish, and others, including Gypsy spoken by women in full Gypsy regalia. Middle-class-appearing men in shirts and ties join the parade, ogling as they go; so do elderly men, usually dressed in their shabby and rumpled Sunday best. The movement of strollers and bike riders is continuous. So is the sound of people and radios blasting loud music. There are groups of teenagers—Anglo, black, and Chicano—sporting vivid tattoos, the latest finery, and the most exaggerated masculinity they can muster. Members of motorcycle clubs wear leather jackets draped with chains and sometimes carry knives in sheaths in their belts. Exaggerated femininity is provided not only by lovely women in bikinis, and by beautiful girls who wear nothing under their tight T-shirts, but also by exaggeratedly gay men who mince by, sometimes hugging and kissing as they go. Whether coming to the beach or leaving it, or merely seeking refreshments, ordinary beachgoers at towers 16 and 15 must pass through, or for a short time join, this crowd.

In 1975 ten separate observations were made of the promenade in an effort to determine how many and what kinds of alarming-appearing people collect there, and what ordinary beachgoers do when they encounter them. We found that a male and female observer could agree quite well in identifying conspicuously strange appearances on the walkway. Two such trials showed only a 15 percent disagreement; in a third, the male and female observer agreed on ten persons, with the male adding two others whom the female missed, and the female adding one whom the male missed. Some inaccuracy in such observations is due to the size of the crowds on the walkway, which make it difficult to see everyone at once. It seems to be the case that male and female observers can independently agree almost all of the time on whether a person is indeed anomalous in appearance. That is no doubt the case, because people in this area can be very anomalous indeed. For example, on one warm weekend afternoon, during a ten-minute period of observation, seven middle-aged to elderly men were seen walking by who exhibited bizarre mannerisms—facial tics, hand flapping, dancing or hopping gaits, chewing on paper or wood, or (in four cases) talking loudly to themselves.

The following is a summary of what the author saw during a 30-minute period in the afternoon of an only moderately crowded weekday. As usual, many foreign languages were being spoken. There were people in all kinds of dress, from relatively formal female attire including high-heeled boots being worn by a woman who would have looked like an aging prostitute, were it not that she seemed too unattractive for that occupation and was dragging a cute little girl by the hand. There were men dressed in shirts, ties, and coats, and there was every other kind of dress imaginable, including a man dressed as a Plains Indian complete with a long feathered war bonnet. There were at least two gangs of three or four teenagers who were obviously on the prowl and were avoided by everyone else on the promenade. All of these people were seen directly across from the volleyball courts, where the most athletically wholesome of people, one would imagine, were totally engrossed in playing or watching volleyball games. Next to them was the grassy area in front of the lifeguard headquarters, where strikingly odd people were often seen. This particular day was no exception.

At the beginning of the 30-minute period of observation, a woman of 60 or so, who appeared to be patently psychotic, came down the promenade, fumblingly purchased lemonade (which cost 40 cents) and then moved onto the grassy area.

She was talking to herself, her toothless mouth chattering audibly, and her hands were fluttering; her ankles were covered with sores and she wore filthy clothing, topped by a dirty, inexpensive coat of a white, thick, furry sort with a hood attached. This pathetic person stood there for a while, finished her lemonade in a gulp, then began to tear up the paper cup into narrow strips, which she threw into a trash can, only to fish some of them back out again. She next picked up a kind of plastic bag and a cloth bag, wandered to the far end of the grassy area where she stood in the shade talking to herself and, waving her arms violently, then moved back to the sunny area where she lay down, but did not sleep. Her hands were moving in a manner that looked like gestures. This woman was sufficiently bizarre that many people took notice of her, yet no one moved away from her, even though quite a number of people were within five to ten yards of her. They did not remove their children from her presence either, but merely looked on with more than usual curiosity. They were intrigued but not frightened.

About the same time a man with very short crewcut hair came walking down the promenade dressed in a business suit and polished leather shoes. By appearance, he could have been a policeman or a businessman or some other quite conservative middle-class person, but as he passed by, his hands suddenly began flitting about in a twitching manner of a sort that would make you think he possessed one of the most massive tics known to psychiatry. He then began talking to himself and capped off the performance by a series of gestures in which his hands flew about his head and his fingers waggled about rapidly. He walked toward the pier and on a couple of occasions he repeated these bizarre gestures and did three little hops—like a rabbit, or a child playing hopscotch. He returned some minutes later in the other direction, picked up a volleyball that was bouncing in his direction, threw it back appropriately, and walked away in the direction from which he had originally come, appearing now to be completely normal. No one appeared to notice him.

A couple then came by, the man looking like a weightlifter

with a nude woman tattooed on his bare back; the woman was a very tough-looking blond who also sported a tattoo, this one on the thigh. From their conversation overheard at the lemonade stand, they must have been illiterate and perhaps were mildly retarded. Neither, for example, could read the menu nor make change adequately. There were also several homosexual men who were quite effeminate, including a young black man who was fervently engaged in an effort to seduce an older white man on a bench in front of the volleyball games. There was also an elderly man with what appeared to be acromegaly. He wore filthy, ragged clothing and he walked slowly along, apparently searching for something of value in trash cans, which he poked about in quite thoroughly.

The final anomalous person seen was a man about 50, wearing a white shirt and bow tie. He looked like an ordinary businessman except that he was toothless. He repeatedly approached young women, staring at their breasts avidly, but as soon as they glanced back at him, he moved away and fixed his eyes on another target. The boyfriend of one woman glared at him, and he scuttled away, but he was back in five minutes, ogling as blatantly as before. Although the individuals would differ somewhat on another day, the picture recorded on this day is characteristic of the amount and quality of strangeness seen on the promenade during a 30-minute period on a pleasant August afternoon.

How did ordinary beachgoers respond to this area and to the strange people in it? The answer is difficult to provide with assurance because we could observe only some outward features of beachgoers' behavior and could seldom hear what they said or know what they felt. Furthermore, even at the level of overt behavior, not all beachgoers reacted in the same way. Even so, there were some striking regularities. Referring to ordinary beachgoers—not to people who live, work, or regularly play volleyball in the immediate area—we found that male beachgoers who went to the promenade acted in a natural, comfortable manner except when approached by members of a teenage "gang," a motorcycle "club," or an exceptionally tough-looking male. Their response in these cases was to step aside and avoid eye contact.

Many female beachgoers said that they avoided the promenade area as much as possible, and quite a few women were observed to avoid the promenade as they came to the beach or left it. These women walked to and from their cars by walking along the sand parallel to the promenade and not crossing over it until they reached a point farther south or north where the crowds are less dense or where, as in the north, the walkway stops altogether. Others who crossed the walkway where it is most crowded did so briskly without making eye contact. Most women who went to that area, whether to cross it or to buy refreshments, usually put a top on over their bathing suits and some put pants on as well. These women not only avoided making eye contact but did not respond to men who said "hello" or otherwise attempted to initiate conversation.

The sense of anxiety felt in this area can be illustrated by an incident in which a woman took her seven-year-old son to a lemonade stand. He placed a small bucket and his fishing pole against the wall of the stand but did not want to leave it there, even though it was in plain sight; he said, "Someone's going to steal it." His mother assured him that no one was going to steal his fishing pole, but she took his hand and held him close to her side until they had the lemonade; they then gathered the boy's pole and bucket and walked away so rapidly that the boy was literally being dragged along. It seemed that her nervousness was as great as his.

Another young woman who regularly goes to the beach at area 16 said succinctly what many other women expressed in somewhat different words: "I really dig this part of the beach, you know. The only thing I don't like about it is all those creepy people on the promenade. They really make me uncomfortable. I'm glad they stay there instead of coming out on the beach." On the other hand, a series of observations in 1975 and 1976 indicated that a substantial minority of women, ranging from 30 to 40 percent of female beachgoers at areas 15 and 16, not only frequent the promenade alone in their bikinis, but do so without any apparent trace of discomfort. Many of these women are young and very attractive. Why these women feel comfortable on the promenade when so many others do not is impossible to say.

## Conclusion

What we saw on the promenade is apparently only an intensified version of what we saw on the sand. Many beachgoers admit that they enjoy people-watching, and strange-appearing people who offer no particular personal threat are either ignored or looked at with open interest. Strange-looking men, however, especially younger ones, are avoided. If they cannot be ignored, the beachgoer moves away discreetly without comment or eye contact.

Something we cannot determine is how many people avoid the promenade or beach areas 15 and 16 altogether because they were once frightened or offended by someone there. We find it difficult to believe that most female beachgoers can be altogether comfortable on or near the promenade, yet the percentage of women in general and single women in particular is the same at areas 15 and 16 as at any other part of the beach. Furthermore, women who were interviewed at areas 15 and 16 (see Chapter Seven) made no greater mention of discomfort than did women at other areas, and they were no more likely than women in other areas to say that anyone's appearance (or conduct) had bothered them. Perhaps this is so because the occurrence of actual trouble in the form of aggression or sexual molestation appears to be relatively infrequent on the promenade. In ten separate observation periods we saw *no* instances of open confrontation of any kind. Annoyed glances and avoiding one another were as far as anything went.

We must suppose from these observations that while some women dislike the area or avoid it, many others find it perfectly congenial, and, just as they do on the sand, are able successfully to tune out of their awareness any threat that anomalous-appearing people might otherwise pose. We must also conclude that the range of normal appearances at Southland Beach is very wide indeed; it takes a particularly strange or menacing person to evoke an alarm reaction in most beachgoers. Unless such a person commits an overtly offensive act or moves too close to a beachgoers' personal territory on the sand, the anomalous person is likely to be tolerated, ignored, or even enjoyed. This is true even at beach areas 15 and 16, where anomalous persons are seen more often than elsewhere on Southland Beach.

The comments of one 28-year-old woman provide a good illustration of beachgoers' tolerance: "I saw an old man walking down the beach with shit all over him. He was covered with it." When asked how she reacted, she said: "I just looked away. Everyone at the beach is into his own thing."

In order to understand this expressed tolerance of strangeness by beachgoers, we next turn to a more detailed consideration of what beachgoers say about their experiences on Southland Beach.

# 7

## More Perspectives on Trouble: Beachgoers' Comments and Police Records

Previous chapters have pointed to an apparent paradox about trouble on Southland Beach. On the one hand, lifeguards and police officers often say that this beach is dangerous, even during the day when it is most crowded, and their daily routines on this beach make it clear that they often encounter more trouble than they can handle. On the other hand, however, observations of beachgoers' behavior made up and down this beach indicate that trouble does not occur very often, and that when it does take place, it is seldom serious.

In order to look more carefully at this apparent contradiction, this chapter will first present the beliefs and attitudes of beachgoers themselves, and then examine the crime records kept by the police. Finally, an attempt will be made to specify how often various kinds of rule violations and ensuing trouble occur on Southland Beach.

### What Beachgoers Think About Trouble on the Beach

To determine what beachgoers felt about beachgoing in general, a series of interviews was conducted in the Los Angeles area. First, some 70 persons were interviewed in public places in Southland City (parks, markets, car washes, bus stops, and the like). Next, questionnaires were distributed in various classrooms of a large university in Los Angeles, and, finally, 40 door-to-door interviews were conducted in each of two neighborhoods, one an upper-middle-class area near the beach and the other a lower-income area in the central city. Despite the heterogeneity of the respondents and the varied conditions under which the information was collected, men and women alike expressed a remarkably uniform set of beliefs and attitudes about beach-going. Thus well over 90 percent of all these persons—whether or not they were beachgoers themselves—characterized the beach in highly positive terms, such as "relaxing," "wholesome," and "healthy." Less than 10 percent expressed any negative views of the beach, and almost all of these persons considered the beach boring or dirty, not unsafe or morally reprehensible.[1] While it would be a mistake to make too much of information collected in this fashion, it is apparently the case that most persons throughout Southern California share a generally positive view of the beach, and almost without exception think of it as being safe.

To explore the attitudes of actual beachgoers, several kinds of interviews were conducted on Southland Beach itself. The first of these sets of interviews was conducted in the summer of 1975 by two women who were asked to speak to all sorts of beachgoers up and down the length of Southland Beach.[2] All areas of the beach were covered, and people of various ages—from 17 to 67—were interviewed. Men and women alone, couples, and family groups were all included, although more women (23) than men (12) actually responded. When a couple or family group was interviewed, it was common for the woman rather than the man to respond, perhaps because the interviewers were also women. Four of the respondents were black, but only one was Chicano. No one refused to be interviewed. We first asked, "What don't you like about the beach?" Eleven people said "nothing;" three mentioned the weather; seven said litter on the sand; four disliked the dirty water or seaweed; three objected to crowded conditions; and seven disliked something about the behavior of other people. In an effort to clarify the annoyance beachgoers might feel about other beachgoers, we then asked: "Is there anything that bothers you about how other people act?" Twenty-one people said that nothing bothered them. Fourteen people mentioned a variety of minor problems—frisbees, people sitting too close to them, loud or obscene teenagers, or kids kicking sand. One 17-year-old girl said that people "often" frightened her. This was the only complaint that seemed to be at all serious. We then asked people if they had ever complained about anything while at the beach. Twenty-nine of the 35 people said they had not. Two women said that they had complained to lifeguards about dogs, three people (two of whom were male) had complained to other beachgoers about throwing footballs or frisbees, and one woman had complained to a lifeguard about the trash on the beach and in the public bathrooms. We next asked if people felt that any of the "beach regulations" should be enforced more strictly, and found the same pattern of response. Twenty-seven people said that everything was all right the way it was, while eight mentioned stricter enforcement involving the same kinds of minor problems—dogs, ballgames, and trash.

We also asked how people felt about police protection on the beach. Sixteen people were positive, ten were negative, and nine were equivocal; in general, older people were more positive than younger ones. Most of the negative reactions took a surprising tone: people said, essentially, that the sight of a police officer would make them think there was something to fear, and would change the beach from a relaxing place to a tense one. As an example of the extent to which beachgoers want to think of the beach as a place that does not *need* police protection, this is a significant answer, as we shall see later. But there is apparently no relationship between actually seeing a police officer on the beach (18 persons had done so) and feeling that the beach is unsafe. It is noteworthy, however, that only one person of the 35 said that she had thought of calling the police (about a man who was masturbating); 34 beachgoers said that they had never thought of doing so.

In an attempt to be more explicit about beach trouble we asked, "Has anything ever angered or frightened you at this beach?" Only eight people said yes. One was a man who was angry because a lifeguard had called him out of the water. The other seven were women, six of whom had been frightened by a man who had followed them, molested them, or exposed themselves to them. Yet only one of these women thought of calling the police. Similarly, when these 35 people were asked, "Is there anytime at the beach when you don't feel safe?" eight people—all women—answered that they were afraid at the beach late in the day, a time when they felt vulnerable to serious harm. Not one beachgoer said that the beach was unsafe during the day.

Despite the many negatively oriented questions that had already been asked, when we asked each beachgoer what would make Southland Beach more enjoyable, 18 people said that the beach was fine the way it was; the 17 who mentioned some improvement spoke only of such matters as cleaning up litter or providing better recreational facilities. Not one beachgoer mentioned anything having to do with the behavior of other people, much less with personal safety.

We do not want to make too much of these interview findings. The sample was taken catch-as-catch can, and the number of persons involved was small. Neither the questions themselves nor our use of them led people to reflect deeply or to expand upon their opinions. The interview was designed only to provide some information for more systematic interviewing later. Despite all its weaknesses, however, this interview made several points. It is clear that most of the beachgoers interviewed enjoy this beach. They were seldom troubled by events or persons at the beach; they were sometimes annoyed, but seldom in any serious or lasting way. Only rarely or under special circumstances was there any expression of concern for their personal safety. However, when concern for personal safety or well-being was expressed, it was done by women. These findings, then, lend support to our ethnographically based conclusion that women feel more vulnerable at the beach than men do. Indeed, one hardly needs an interview to demonstrate that, in almost every conceivable way, women *are* more vulnerable at the beach than men are. What may be significant is the suggestion that whereas women are more aware of trouble and danger than men are, *most* women nevertheless regard Southland Beach as a peaceful, relaxing, trouble-free place.

To explore further how women at Southland Beach feel about beachgoing, another set of questions was formulated. It was hoped that these questions would elicit more complete and thoughtful answers, and present a more balanced interest in positive and negative aspects of beachgoing.[3] In order to maximize the probability that the women interviewed would indeed think of themselves as vulnerable, the interview was confined to women who were on the beach without male escorts. From our observations, it was clear that women often came to the beach alone, with small children, or with other women. We attempted to locate equal numbers of women in each of these categories, but since we also wanted to sample equal numbers of women in the more heterogeneous and presumably less troublesome areas, we actually interviewed 26 women who were alone on the beach, 23 who were with other women, and 17 who were with small children.[4] The original intent was to interview 30 women in each of these categories, but because of the consistency of the answers, interviewing was terminated after the completion of 66 interviews. Because neither black women nor Chicanas very often come to Southland Beach unless they are with a male or a family group, only seven women who were not Anglos were interviewed.

The interview was conducted in the summer of 1975 by the same interviewers as before. They approached women who fell into their quota categories, introduced the study as one that was interested in how people felt about the beach, and added that the questions would only take a few minutes. In fact, the interview averaged about 15 minutes, ranging from as little as 10 minutes to as long as 30 minutes. Only three women refused to be interviewed. At the end of the interview, a few women asked what the interview was all about, and they were given as full an answer as they cared to listen to. No one seemed in the least upset by the interview and quite a few seemed to enjoy it, talking casually for some time after the interview itself had been completed. The interviewers had a subjective impression that these women were more interested in this interview than in the preliminary one; and it is clear that the answers to this interview were somewhat longer. As before, the answers were internally consistent.

The 66 women interviewed ranged in age from 13 to 58, with an average age of 31. Only 21 of these women were married, despite the fact that only ten were 18 years of age or younger. We did not ask about divorces, although two women volunteered this information, but from the tenor of the interviews it would appear that many of these single women were divorced. Women at the beach with children and those at the beach with friends had the same average age. Women who came to the beach alone were slightly older (average 34.5) and only four of these 26 women were married. In general, then, more than two-thirds of these women were single (47 of 66); their average age was about the same (29 years) as that of the married women. Like their counterparts in the first interview who traveled an average of 19 miles one way to the beach, these 66 women averaged 20 miles one way, and most of them came to the beach often. Over half of the 66 women said that they came to the beach at least once a week during the summer. Women who came to the beach alone did so somewhat more often than other women, with more than half of them visiting the beach even more frequently than once a week. But nine women who came to Southland Beach alone were infrequent beachgoers, averaging only a few trips per year. It is also worth noting that most of these women have been coming to Southland Beach for a long time. These 66 women have been coming to the beach for an average of 13 years, the same average reported by women who came to the beach alone.

After asking about the frequency of beachgoing and the distance traveled, the women were asked, "What do you like best about the beach?" As we expected, their answers emphasized sun, water, fresh air, and relaxation. Most often mentioned (37 times) was the sun and getting a tan. Three married women mentioned getting away from home; two other women mentioned people-watching, and two teenagers said that what they liked best about the beach was "guys." As before, more than half of the women said that they swam at least occasionally. We then asked if they ever came to the beach early or late in the day. It is a bit surprising that seven women, including three married women, said that they did, and two others said that they "might." A few said that they used to, but that it was no longer safe.

After several questions about pleasant experiences on Southland Beach we asked whether anything "really unpleasant" had happened. Twenty-eight of the 66 women said that they had suffered something unpleasant. The two most trivial experiences involved women who had had sand kicked in their faces. There was one mention of severe sunburn, one jellyfish sting, and one severely cut arm. Four women had had trouble in the water, three saying that they had almost drowned. Another had found a dead dog floating by her in the water as she tried to swim. One woman mentioned being on the beach one morning when lifeguards found the body of a man in the parking lot; he had committed suicide during the night. The other unpleasant experiences involved interpersonal relations that were actually or potentially serious. In the least serious of these, a woman was approached by a panhandler who cursed her when she gave him nothing. Two other women were frightened by men whom they referred to as "weird"—one of these men was blind. One woman was frightened by a group of drug-intoxicated teenagers; she complained to a lifeguard, who asked them to leave. When the teenagers refused to do so, this woman grabbed her children and left the beach. Three women were concerned about "rowdy" males, mostly teenagers, who had either engaged in a brawl or threatened to. Three women mentioned being offended by men who either masturbated toward them or attempted to grab them in a sexually aggressive manner. Six women complained about being bothered—"hassled" was the most common term—by men who were trying to pick them up. Two women were not specific about their unpleasant experiences. There were no significant differences between women at the beach alone and those not alone in terms of either the kind or the number of unpleasant experiences reported.

We then asked, "Is there anything that annoys you at the beach?" We hoped that this question would shift the women's thoughts from occasional unpleasant incidents to more common annoyances. Thirty-nine of the women said that something did annoy them. Three once again complained about men "hassling" them; four were annoyed by necking. Twelve mentioned annoyances such as litter, dogs, crowding, frisbees, drunks, seaweed, and the like. Four others were annoyed by football games. The largest number, fifteen, mentioned children running and kicking sand on them. It seems to be the case, then, that everyday annoyances, while common, are not very serious. It should also be noted that 27 women, eight of whom had reported a rather serious unpleasant experience, said that they were not usually annoyed by anything.

After various questions about hypothetical responses to various sorts of trouble, we asked, "Do you remember seeing anyone whose appearance or behavior on the beach bothered you?" After our onslaught of questions about trouble, we expected that this question would evoke affirmative answers from almost all the women. Instead, 39 women said that they had not seen anyone whose appearance or behavior had bothered them. In looking back through the earlier responses of these women, we found that 13 of them had earlier said that they had been bothered by someone. Perhaps the phrasing of the question suggested *appearance* more than behavior, because women who answered affirmatively identified people who were psychotic (5), drunk (5), mentally retarded (4), nude (3), dirty (3), and overweight (2), among other things. Be this as it may, what is most significant is the number of women who throughout the entire interview denied seeing or experiencing anything or anyone on the beach that was annoying or unpleasant. There were 23 such women and there was nothing about their age, marital status, frequency of beachgoing, attractiveness, location on the beach, or reason for coming to the beach that distinguished them from the other 43 women.

We also asked "What would you like to change about the beach to make it a more enjoyable place?" Only three women mentioned anything having to do with other beachgoers: one wanted "pick-up artists" chased off the beach, and two others said non-specifically that the beach should be made less dangerous for women. But twenty women said that nothing should be done, that the beach satisfied them just as it was. The remainder pointed to changes that had nothing to do with personal safety. For example, many wanted a cleaner beach, or more doors installed in the public bathrooms. Others wanted a nude beach, a beach they could bring their dogs to, or free parking. A few wanted better restaurants or playground facilities for children. One pretty 22-year-old said that she wished the beach would be made legal for "dope smoking." Despite our many questions about trouble between people on the beach, when it came to suggesting changes, virtually no interest was expressed in clearing the beach of its strange or annoying persons, nor in providing better police or lifeguard protection.

For the most part, these 66 women repeated the responses of the 35 people who were interviewed earlier. Most were annoyed by a few things and a sizeable minority could recall unpleasant experiences. Yet few seemed to be seriously troubled by anything that they had witnessed or experienced at the beach. In fact, about one-third of these women said that nothing about the beach or other beachgoers ever bothered them.

We had thought that these women who came to Southland Beach without men might perceive it as a more-or-less frightening place. This did not prove to be the case. First, there were no appreciable differences in attitudes between women who visited the presumably most troublesome parts of the beach (just north or south of the pier) and those who visited the presumably more trouble-free areas. Nor was there any difference relating to age. Finally, whether women saw the beach as troublesome or peaceful was not related to whether they came to the beach alone, with children, or with other women.

In the summer of 1976 an additional 41 interviews were completed with unescorted women on Southland Beach. The answers given in 1976 were in no significant way different from those obtained in 1975. In addition, 51 women who frequently visited Southland Beach were interviewed at length by several interviewers, both male and female. Some of these interviews took place on the beach, others at the womens' homes. These interviews will be discussed in greater detail in Chapter Nine, but for now the important point is that these long interviews, which explored all aspects of a woman's experience of going to Southland Beach, strongly confirm the results of the earlier interview: women see this beach as a pleasant, relaxing, and safe place. They recognize minor annoyances and know that unpleasant experiences, especially involving the sexual attentions of men, can also occur. But they remain convinced that Southland Beach is for them an altogether safe place. In fact, they react with indignation or disbelief if it is suggested to them that their sense of peace and safety might be illusory.

## Police Records of Crime on Southland Beach

It is impossible to look upon police crime records as accurate reflections of the amount of trouble on Southland Beach. The one thing that can be said with confidence is that these records greatly *underestimate* actual crime on the beach. As we have seen, even if all the officers patrolled in identical fashion—and all were perfect instruments of law enforcement—neither Unit 99 nor a foot patrol could possibly observe or respond to more than a fraction of what occurs on the beach on any given day. Moreover, as we have also seen, most beachgoers are reluctant to complain about anything, preferring to ignore trouble. Even when complaints are made, some lifeguards are reluctant to pass them on to the police. Finally, even when a violation of the law comes to the attention of a police officer, this violation may be ignored or handled by a warning rather than become a statistic in the form of an FI, citation, or arrest.

We must conclude, therefore, that crime on the beach—particularly minor crime such as dog violations, drunkenness, petty theft, indecent exposure, or even fights—is far more common than police records could possibly indicate. How much more common is anyone's guess, but a factor of four or five would be conservative, and one of twenty or more not unlikely for some offenses. Even serious crimes of violence, such as molesting women or rape, are vastly under-reported. Perhaps the only crime not under-reported is homicide. Needless to say, none of this is news to the police, in Southland City or anywhere else.[5] Keeping in mind that crime reports are underestimates of actual crime, let us examine these records for what they can tell us about the nature, the location, and to a lesser extent, the frequency of crime on Southland Beach.

The Southland City Police Department maintains several kinds of records that provide information about crime on the beach. First there are records concerning the beach patrols of Unit 99. Each officer assigned to Unit 99 maintains a log of his activities. These logs are summarized by the SCPD in monthly memos, as shown in Table 2. There are several noteworthy aspects to these records. It is obvious, for example, that some statistics have little to do with the time of the year or the number of beach patrols carried out. On the other hand, misdemeanor arrests rise sharply during the summer months of June, July, and August, and FI's (Field Interrogations of suspicious persons) are more numerous during the summer as well. Felony arrests are far less subject to seasonal fluctuations.

The totals shown in Table 2 may give us some idea of the magnitude of illegal activity at the beach. For example, there were 52 felony arrests during the year. They also tell us that there is no invariant relationship between the number of patrols conducted and the number of "statistics" generated.

There were approximately the same numbers of patrols each month from May through January, but there were major fluctuations in the number of arrests and citations. Thus during 1975 there were 152 FI's in January and only 40 in December, and there were 62 misdemeanor arrests in August, but only 11 in January. Dog and traffic citations also varied markedly from month to month, suggesting that if there is a quota system that guides officers at the beach, then it does not operate very predictably.

The SCPD maintains no other tabulations of beach crime as distinct from crime elsewhere in the city. However, they do routinely file a report for every incident that involves a misdemeanor or felony throughout the city. By examining each of these reports it was possible for us to obtain a more complete picture of crime at the beach.[6] Unlike the beach patrol reports, which refer only to actual citations or arrests, these statistics include all reported crimes whether an arrest was made or not. These reports also show that criminal activity comes to the attention of the police most often during the summer months. In February 1975, for example, there were 18 crime reports at the beach, and in March 1975, there were 19. In July, on the other hand, there were 50 reports, and in August, there were 34 (the same differential between winter and summer months was found in 1974 and 1976 as well). It should be kept in mind, of course, that despite the lesser frequency of crime reports in winter months, serious crimes can occur at that time. In March 1975, for example, there were three assaults with intent to murder, one assault against a police officer, and a rape.

There were 102 such crime reports for the months of July through September of 1975, and 114 for the same period in 1976, the two summers when our observations of the beach took place. In 1975, a total of 58 of these occurred during daylight hours (59 in 1976), 28 at night (40 in 1976), and the rest during dawn or twilight hours (five crime reports in 1975 and 12 in 1976 were not specific regarding the time of occurrence). Thirty-one of these incidents (30 in 1976) took place on the sandy beach itself; 71 (84 in 1976) occurred in parking lots,

**Table 2**
Results of Beach Patrols by Unit 99 for 1975
(from SCPD)

| | January | February | March | April | May | June | July | August | September | October | November | December |
|---|---|---|---|---|---|---|---|---|---|---|---|---|
| Estimated beach attendance | 253,900 | 138,500 | 296,200 | 185,525 | 727,750 | 898,000 | 3,744,000 | 2,341,000 | 824,500 | 260,750 | 191,500 | 98,850 |
| Number of beach patrols | 178 | 106 | 147 | 147 | 213 | 229 | 195 | 211 | 228 | 212 | 186 | 182 |
| Felony arrests | 4 | 1 | 1 | 3 | 4 | 5 | 5 | 6 | 2 | 13 | 3 | 5 |
| Misdemeanor arrests | 11 | 6 | 7 | 14 | 14 | 36 | 47 | 62 | 20 | 32 | 15 | 12 |
| Immigration arrests | 0 | 0 | 1 | 0 | 0 | 0 | 6 | 4 | 3 | 0 | 0 | 0 |
| Found lost child | 0 | 0 | 3 | 6 | 7 | 4 | 7 | 5 | 4 | 3 | 2 | 5 |
| Traffic citation | 0 | 0 | 12 | 14 | 16 | 22 | 52 | 50 | 22 | 23 | 34 | 44 |

| | | | | | | | | | | | | |
|---|---|---|---|---|---|---|---|---|---|---|---|---|
| Dogs impounded | 11 | 6 | 6 | 2 | 3 | 9 | 11 | 17 | 45 | 16 | 3 | 5 |
| Citations for dogs | 225 | 105 | 129 | 111 | 57 | 38 | 107 | 62 | 78 | 95 | 55 | 77 |
| Citations for drinking | 1 | 3 | 0 | 0 | 0 | 0 | 5 | 11 | 5 | 1 | 0 | 0 |
| Citations for sleeping | 4 | 0 | 0 | 0 | 0 | 0 | 2 | 11 | 13 | 0 | 0 | 0 |
| Citations for fireworks | 0 | 0 | 0 | 0 | 0 | 0 | 11 | 0 | 0 | 0 | 0 | 0 |
| Citations for fire on beach | 1 | 0 | 0 | 0 | 0 | 1 | 0 | 0 | 0 | 0 | 0 | 0 |
| Citations, other | 0 | 0 | 0 | 0 | 0 | 0 | 2 | 4 | 2 | 1 | 1 | 0 |
| FI cards[a] | 152 | 21 | 52 | 70 | 95 | 138 | 146 | 135 | 122 | 67 | 84 | 40 |

[a]Field interrogation reports.

bathrooms, the promenade, or other locations on the fringe around the beach. Table 3 presents further information regarding the nature, time, and place of these incidents.

From inspection of this table, it is immediately apparent that by far the most commonly detected criminal activity involves theft of one kind or another. Assault is the next most common crime, but it is infrequent by comparison. Neither alcoholic nor narcotic intoxication is at all common, and indecent exposure is only rarely reported. The majority of all crime reports, including violent crime, occurred during the daylight hours, but twice as many incidents occurred on the fringe area around the beach as on the sand itself. Whether this reflects a greater frequency of crime in fringe areas, or a greater willingness of people in those areas to make complaints, cannot be determined. Both factors are probably involved. We should also note that whereas the number of beach crimes remained remarkably constant in the summers of 1975 and 1976 (102 and 114), there were some dramatic differences in the kinds of crimes reported from one summer to the next. Thus burglary or strongarm theft was reduced from 20 instances in 1975 to only 13 in 1976, while petty theft and assault both increased greatly in 1976.

Crimes of violence sometimes occurred during the summers of 1975 and 1976. In 1975, for example, there were 14 assaults, five of which involved the use of a deadly weapon, and one rape. Five of these assaults took place in broad daylight. A homicide took place at night in late June of 1975; a homosexual male was killed by a blow on the head around midnight and his companion received serious head injuries. A woman was shot in the head and left for dead at 10:30 one evening; miraculously, she survived. In comparison, there were only nine homicides in all of Southland City in 1975.

Deadly weapons were carried onto the beach, even during the day, during the summer of 1975. For example, at two in the afternoon, a man was seen walking up and down the promenade with a pistol in his waistband; when he sat down for a beer, a call to the police was made by a store owner and he was arrested. At dawn a few days later, a man was ap-

**Table 3**
Crime Reports for Summers of 1975 and 1976
(July, August, and September)

| Type of Offense | Total | | Time of Offense | | | | | | | | Location of Offense | | | |
| --- | --- | --- | Day | | Night | | Twilight | | Unknown | | Sand | | Fringe | |
| | 1975 | 1976 | 1975 | 1976 | 1975 | 1976 | 1975 | 1976 | 1975 | 1976 | 1975 | 1976 | 1975 | 1976 |
| Petty theft | 17 | 41 | 14 | 36 | 1 | 3 | 2 | 1 | 0 | 1 | 10 | 19 | 7 | 22 |
| Burglary, strongarm theft | 30 | 13 | 15 | 1 | 9 | 9 | 3 | 2 | 3 | 1 | 9 | 2 | 21 | 11 |
| Theft from auto | 23 | 17 | 14 | 7 | 3 | 8 | 4 | 2 | 2 | 0 | 0 | 0 | 22 | 17 |
| Assault | 14 | 25 | 7 | 7 | 6 | 14 | 1 | 2 | 0 | 2 | 3 | 5 | 11 | 20 |
| Intoxication or narcotics | 6 | 6 | 2 | 1 | 4 | 3 | 0 | 2 | 0 | 0 | 3 | 1 | 3 | 5 |
| Indecent exposure | 2 | 0 | 2 | 0 | 0 | 0 | 0 | 0 | 0 | 0 | 1 | 0 | 1 | 0 |
| Other | 10 | 12 | 4 | 7 | 5 | 3 | 1 | 0 | 0 | 2 | 5 | 3 | 5 | 9 |
| Total | 102 | 114 | 58 | 59 | 28 | 40 | 11 | 9 | 5 | 6 | 31 | 30 | 70 | 84 |

prehended sleeping under lifeguard tower 15 with his rifle and Bowie knife in plain view. Violence also occurs at night, and can be deadly. For example, there were several reports of gunfire during summer nights. In one of these incidents a 57-year-old man lying in the sand near tower 15 at ten in the evening began to fire a handgun at, among others, a Harbor Patrol officer. When this officer called for the SCPD airplane to illuminate the area, the plane was also fired upon. After firing at citizens and cars on the pier, the suspect was tackled and disarmed by two SCPD officers who had crept up on him from behind. In an even more dangerous incident, a veritable fusillade of shots was fired. At 1:30 A.M. a citizen who was walking along the beach flagged an SCPD patrol car to say that he had just been fired at. When the officer investigated, he too was shot at from the sand. Before the mêlée was over, over 500 shots were fired at officers of the SCPD and other police departments that were drawn to the sound of warfare. Two citizens had been robbed at gunpoint (of $2.25) before the shooting began, but astonishingly no one was injured by gunfire, even though nearby buildings, trash cans, and parked cars were riddled. Six teenagers from the inner city, including three girls, were arrested.

In the summer of 1976, there was somewhat more reported violence than in 1975. For example, there was one rape, one assault with intent to rape, and 23 other assaults, 10 of which involved the use of a deadly weapon. Seven of these assaults took place during daylight hours, between 10 A.M. and 7 P.M.

Violent sexual crimes also occur. For example, in 1975 there were half as many reported rapes at the beach (6) as there were indecent exposures (13). However, while all the reported indecent exposures occurred during the day, often on the sandy beach—as one might expect—only two of the six rapes took place during the day, and only one of these occurred on the sand.

Reports of indecent exposure vary greatly in their details. Most are cases of "flashing" in which a man exposes himself and sometimes masturbates, without directly soliciting or approaching any woman. This is not always true, however. In one incident on a crowded Sunday afternoon, a 21-year-old woman was standing in line at a snack shop waiting to buy her lunch. She felt something poking her from behind. After several times moving away from the source of the poking, she turned to discover that it was a man's erect penis. She ran, then made her complaint to the police. Although this episode is humorous because of the man's absurd openness, it was also frightening, and perhaps even dangerous. Another perhaps more dangerous incident involved a young man who approached several young women on the beach, asking them for sexual relations, then threatening them with rape when they refused. It is obvious that these 13 reported instances of indecent exposure represent only a miniscule percentage of all the similar acts which took place at the beach. As we shall see, women seldom make formal complaints about indecent exposure.

It is also likely that many rapes at the beach, as elsewhere, go unreported. Many of the others that are reported are reduced to the charge of "annoying women." The six rapes reported at Southland Beach in 1975 constitute 13 percent of all rapes in Southland City during that year. The figures were similar in 1974, when the seven reported beach rapes were 19 percent of the annual total in Southland City.[7] Two of the beach rapes in 1974, by the way, took place during the day. One woman was dragged into a car in a beach parking lot and raped at 3:30 P.M. on a crowded July afternoon. Another woman was raped on the sand at 7 P.M. in the early twilight of another summer day when many persons were still on the beach. In both cases there were no known witnesses.

Police departments everywhere are well aware that citizen's complaints all too seldom give them the grounds to take decisive action, and police officers obviously are too few in number to see very much criminal activity while it is actually taking place. One device which helps to fill the gap is the Field Interrogation report, or FI. In many cases, the officer involved will fill out a brief report on a suspicious person including such details as age, sex, ethnicity, place of residence, and the nature of the suspicious activity. It cannot be assumed that every person whom the police "FI" either has committed a crime or will some day do so. Some persons stopped and "FI'd" by the police are innocent of any wrong-doing or any intent to commit a crime. But as we saw in Chapter Four, SCPD officers usually have good reasons for stopping someone and writing up an FI, and many persons who could be FI'd with good reason are not. Any record of FI's, then, is both a distortion and an underestimate of poten-tial criminal activity, but an examination of FI's can neverthe-less yield additional information about the amount and kind of trouble that takes place at the beach.

As with arrest records, the SCPD keeps no file that sepa-rates FI's at the beach from FI's anywhere else in the city. Once again, the complete file of FI's for Southland City had to be reviewed in order to identify FI's that were written at Southland Beach. In the summer months of 1975 (July, Au-gust, and September), 663 FI's were filled out at the beach. Of these 663 suspicious persons, 128 (19 percent) were from Southland City. Another 100 were from nearby areas roughly three to twelve miles distant; the remainder lived many miles distant, including 67 who were residents of other counties, states, or countries. The places of residence of suspicious per-sons, then, do not differ appreciably from those of ordinary beachgoers, except for the fact that 74 of the 663 persons who were FI'd were transients—that is, persons with no reported or reportable residence.

Eighty-eight percent of the FI's involved males; only 12 percent involved females. Ethnic identity did not differ sig-nificantly between males and females. Among all FI's, 57 percent were "Caucasian," 25 percent were "Mexican-American," and 16 percent were "Negro," with "Asians," "Native Americans," and other minorities making up the re-mainder. There are no reliable published data concerning the ethnicity of ordinary beachgoers; our own observations pro-vide estimates for the entire beachfront of 85 percent "Cauca-sian," 5 to 7 percent "Mexican-American," 3 to 5 percent "Negro," with the remainder being persons of other ethnic groups, mostly Asian. If our estimates are correct, both

"Mexican-Americans" and "Negroes" are overrepresented in FI's, as is the case in most Southern California crime statistics. In the summer of 1974, when only 259 FI's were written, the residences of persons FI'd were approximately the same, as was the male-female percentage, but a higher percentage of "Caucasians" (65 percent) was FI'd compared to the other ethnic groups ("Mexican-Americans" 22 percent, "Negroes" 13 percent).

Of the 663 FI's written in the summer of 1975, 353 were written at night, 241 during the day, and 68 during twilight hours. The majority (383) were written in fringe areas; 280 occurred on the sandy beach; two were in unknown locations. Table 4 summarizes the nature, place, and time of all these FI's. The overwhelming majority are written for "suspicious persons," who may be loitering, panhandling, offending other citizens, trespassing, or merely looking out of place. Such persons are FI'd most often at night and on the beach fringe, where their very presence at night can be suspicious. The next largest category—intoxication—requires no explanation. Unlike suspicious persons, intoxicated persons are

**Table 4**

Field Interrogations for Summer 1975

| Reason for Interrogation | Total | Time | | | Place | |
|---|---|---|---|---|---|---|
| | | Day | Night | Twilight | Sand | Fringe |
| Suspicious person, loitering, etc. | 337 | 95 | 206 | 36 | 101 | 236 |
| Alcohol or narcotics intoxication | 97 | 49 | 35 | 13 | 63 | 34 |
| Sleeping | 78 | 15 | 56 | 7 | 60 | 18 |
| Disturbing the peace | 73 | 40 | 32 | 1 | 20 | 53 |
| Sex related | 39 | 23 | 13 | 3 | 22 | 17 |
| Mental illness | 14 | 9 | 3 | 2 | 6 | 8 |
| Dogs | 12 | 9 | 1 | 2 | 6 | 6 |
| Other | 13 | 1 | 7 | 5 | 2 | 11 |
| Total | 663 | 241 | 353 | 69 | 280 | 383 |

most often FI'd during the day and on the sand. People who
sleep illegally do so most often at night, and on the sand,
where it is relatively warm and soft. "Disturbing the peace,"
like "suspicious persons," is a catch-all category. It usually
refers to people who shout or scream or loudly bother others,
but it could also refer to a male annoying a female or to an
intoxicated individual. Such activity occurs about as often at
night as in the day, and most often in fringe areas such as
the pier and walkway. Such people may or may not be intoxicated as well. There were surprisingly few specifically
"sex-related" FI's (annoying women, lewd conduct, child molesting, or homosexual offenses), but the majority of these
violations took place during the day and on the sand, where
people were three times more likely to be FI'd for any reason
than on the fringe. People FI'd for suspected mental illness
are reported primarily during the day, as are people who are
suspected of dog violations. FI's in the "other" category,
which embraces such oddities as planting a bomb on the
beach and throwing a baseball at a police officer, are primarily
night-time occurrences, as, of course, are curfew violations
by juveniles. Although there were 112 fewer FI's in 1976 (551
compared to 663 in 1975), there were no statistically significant differences between 1975 and 1976 concerning either the
kinds of persons involved or the activities that made them
suspicious.

The interpretation of these police statistics is problematic
for all the reasons already mentioned, but some points are
clear. First, South beach is more likely than North beach to
yield crime statistics. Thus 66 percent of all crime reports in
1975 (86 percent in 1976) and 82 percent of all FI's (85 percent
in 1976) occurred on the beach fringe around the pier or on
the beach south of the pier. There is also a clear indication
that violence is more common on South beach. For example,
of 14 arrests for assault with a deadly weapon, 13 occurred on
South beach, and of 18 persons FI'd on suspicion of assault,
16 were on South beach. In the summer of 1976 there were 12
arrests for assault with a deadly weapon and 20 persons were

FI'd on suspicion of assault; all these arrests and FI's took place on South beach. We should note that these differences are not a function of disproportionate patrol activity on South beach; Unit 99 spends as much routine patrol time on North beach as it does on South beach. Second, serious crimes of violence are more common at night than during the day. Finally, day or night, more trouble which becomes known to the police takes place on the fringe of the beach (which includes parking lots and the promenade) than on the sand itself.

### Conclusion: How Much Trouble is There?

Beachgoers themselves say that this beach is pleasant and safe, and our observations bear out their views. Police crime statistics, on the other hand, support police and lifeguard opinion that serious trouble does occur on Southland Beach. In order to provide the best possible estimate of the frequency of serious rule violations on Southland Beach, we made use of police records, our direct participation in police patrols, lifeguard reports and logs, accounts of beachgoers, and our own direct observations. Using all of these sources of information we can offer some estimates about the occurrence of crime on the beach during the peak crowding hours of 10 A.M. and 4 P.M. during the summer. Petty theft (of a radio, wallet, or beach gear) probably occurs three to five times a day on the sandy beach, and even more often on the fringe of the beach. These thefts are seldom reported. Thefts from parked cars are less frequent, probably occurring only once every two or three days, and most of these are reported. Strong-arm thefts—usually purse snatching—are confined primarily to the promenade or the area around the pier. One such daylight crime can be expected every four or five days during the summer; they are usually reported.

Women are sexually accosted or molested with some frequency, and these misdemeanor crimes are rarely reported. We estimate that there are at least three or four such crimes every day (usually indecent exposure, less frequently physical molestation). Indecent exposure occurs all along the beach and its fringe, but sexual assault is probably most common in the parking areas or the public bathrooms.

Reported crimes of violence are almost exclusively confined to South beach and the promenade. Some of these involve the use of deadly weapons, usually a knife. But assaults, especially fist fights, have occurred on North beach as well, and many of these go unreported. We would estimate that some sort of assault, usually a fight involving two young persons or family members, occurs every other day during the summer. Aggravated assault (with a deadly weapon or intent to kill) probably does not occur more often than once every two weeks. Rape is probably even less common, but rape attempts do take place even during the crowded part of the day. We would estimate that there are eight or ten attempted rapes on the sandy beach or its fringe every summer during the peak crowding hours. These sexual assaults are often not reported.

When one considers that there will be 50,000 people on the beach during a cool, overcast summer day and upwards of 300,000 on a warm Sunday, these rates of criminal conduct do not seem extreme. In fact, it seems highly unlikely that very many beachgoers will personally witness a serious crime. As we have determined by direct observation, the trouble that typically happens on the beach is likely to be trivial. Since Southland Beach is a public setting in which serious trouble could easily occur often, we must begin to consider what factors are at work in making this beach a relatively pleasant and safe place.

# 8

## Neutralizing Trouble: The Mellow World of Beachgoers

There can be little doubt that the efforts of the lifeguards and the police play a part in reducing both the frequency and seriousness of trouble on Southland Beach. Just how important these efforts are is an issue that will be taken up in the final chapter. But it is clear that however important the activities of the lifeguards and police may be in making the beach safe and pleasant, these activities are only part of the story. Through their beliefs and their behaviors beachgoers themselves are instrumental in making Southland Beach a relatively trouble-free place. In this chapter, we will consider those beliefs and behaviors, and how they serve to reduce and neutralize trouble.

### Defining the Beach as a Relaxing and Safe Place

Beachgoers, both male and female, say that they come to Southland Beach to enjoy its sun, water, and fresh air. Many say that they want to tan themselves; a few mention people-watching or girl-watching, but almost everyone says that the beach is a place where people go to relax. As we have already seen, almost everyone, whether a frequent beachgoer or not, expresses this view of the beach. This belief actually has two complementary components: first, that beachgoers

go to the beach because they *want* to have a relaxing experience, and second, that the beach environment with its fresh
air, warm sun, and rhythmic surf, actually *produces* relaxation. In every interview conducted on Southland Beach or
with people who often went to this beach, relaxation was
mentioned. Some of these answers stressed the desire of
beachgoers for a relaxing day at the beach, while others emphasized the effect of the beach itself in bringing about relaxation. Many of those interviewed specifically said that
beachgoers were able to get along with one another because
they shared a common interest in relaxation.

For example, in the interview conducted on the beach with
66 women who were without male escorts, we asked: "Since
we're all strangers at the beach, really, why do you think it is
possible for us to get along together?" Only two women said
that beachgoers did not in fact get along together, and only
four women said that they did not know. Both of these
answers, we had thought, would be common. Instead, 60 of
the women gave thoughtful and apparently confident
answers which served to explain why beachgoers did indeed
get along. More remarkable still, these 60 explanations fell
into only two categories—first, that people had a common
interest in relaxed enjoyment, and second, that they minded
their own business. Thus 37 of these women said that
beachgoers got along with one another because they go to the
beach determined to have a peaceful, relaxing time. Several
of these women said that the beach environment produces a
soothing feeling, but others emphasized the role that people
themselves play in creating a relaxed atmosphere. A married
woman said, "Everybody comes here to mellow out. I can't
imagine anything bad happening." These kinds of remarks
were typical: "The beach can wash away problems." "The
beach puts everyone in a good mood." "The beach is special;
everyone's so relaxed. Something magical happens to
everyone." "People come here to relax, no one's looking for
trouble." "It's so mellow and laid back here, my mind just
goes on its own trip." "The ocean and the sun calm everyone
down; the sun is really so debilitating that all you can do is

relax." "When I get down on the warm sand, and listen to the surf and feel the lovely breeze, all my worries and anxieties fade away; when everyone is feeling like that how could there possibly be any trouble?" "There's a general air of, uh, relaxation I guess. Not really camaraderie, but much less dog-eat-dog than real life. People just leave you alone."

The remaining 23 women saw matters somewhat differently, as this last comment implies. They said that beachgoers were able to get along with one another because they stay to themselves, "minding their own business." This is an important consideration that will be taken up later, but before doing so it is important to emphasize the extent to which beachgoers think of Southland Beach as a "safe" place. We have already seen in Chapter Seven that very few beachgoers think of this beach—or any other—as being unsafe. Again and again, they said they were sure that nothing really serious could possibly happen "in broad daylight and in front of so many people." Indeed, many of the women we interviewed added that they thought of this beach as being among the safest of places they knew in their urban experience. As a 25-year-old woman with a Master's Degree put it, "It may be one of the few places a woman can go to be alone and yet feel safe from actual physical harm." The most common kind of answer given was typified by this 27-year-old woman: "I can't understand why people wouldn't feel safe at the beach, because there are other bodies there. What could happen to you in broad daylight on the beach?" A man in his thirties said this: "What could happen here? I feel safer here than I do at home." Another man in his thirties added: "I've never seen anything bad here. I think the beach dissipates peoples' anger. I know it does mine. Anyway, with all these people around, what kind of trouble could there be?"

The sentiment that the beach is safe during the day, particularly because it is crowded, is almost universally expressed by beachgoers, especially by women. "There's safety in numbers" is no idle shibboleth for beachgoers; it is an essential feature of their beach reality. As we shall see later in this chapter, this belief in the safety of numbers is not always borne out by observations of beach behavior; but beachgoers not only express this belief with the utmost conviction, they behave as if the beach were indeed perfectly safe, at least when others are around. Like victims of muggers (Lejeune and Alex 1973) who are surprised after being mugged, beachgoers express a strong sense of security, interpersonal trust, and inviolability.

Our observations confirm that most beachgoers behave as if the beach were a perfectly safe place. They come to the beach alone or with small children, they undress in the full view of others, they lie down and go to sleep, and many of them even leave their possessions on their towels when they go for a swim. With a very few exceptions, the thousands of beachgoers who assemble on Southland Beach give every indication that they are indeed relaxed, content, and secure.

As a substantial number of beachgoers themselves pointed out, the relaxed, peaceful, and safe quality of Southland Beach is not solely a product of beachgoers' shared beliefs that matters couldn't be otherwise. It is also related to the observable fact that beachgoers stay to themselves, avoiding interaction with strangers. As was mentioned earlier in this chapter, 23 women of the 66 questioned said that people were able to get along with one another for the very reason that they had nothing whatever to do with one another. Almost everyone interviewed during the years of this research recognized that the isolation of beachgoers from one another was a fact of beach life.

### Establishing Personal Territory

The first thing beachgoers do when they arrive on the sandy beach is claim a patch of sand as their own. They mark this territory with a beach towel or a blanket, as well as with their beach gear and whatever clothing they remove. The territory marked by the towel, as well as the sand surrounding it for five or six feet on all sides, becomes the personal space or private territory of the person or persons who come to the beach together.[1] For anyone to walk over this space or to sit down within it without being invited to do so would be

Beachgoers walking near area 15.

a major affront. Such intrusions, in fact, rarely occur, being confined almost entirely to children who sometimes run across someone's space or to men who enter a woman's territory in an attempt to make a "pick-up"—and as we shall see, even men intent on a pick-up are usually careful not to invade a woman's private territory. In claiming a personal territory, beachgoers rarely place their towel within six feet of another person's towel. When this happens, as is most likely to occur in the case of Chicano families who appear to think of proximity on the beach in more intimate terms, the beachgoer whose territory has been "invaded" is likely to express annoyance and to move away without delay.

With only a handful of exceptions, all of the beachgoers whom we interviewed were explicit about their belief that they and others claimed a personal territory at the beach and that this territory was, and should be, private and inviolable.

These words are characteristic of men and women alike: "When I get to the beach I pick out my little plot of sand and set down my towel. For the next few hours that is my own little world; it belongs to me." Many added that once a beachgoer claimed a territory, he or she entered his or her private psychological experience. These comments, one by a man, the other by a woman, were commonplace: "Everyone is in his own private dream world," and "Everyone has his own little territory and is on his own trip."

The following comments were made when a woman research associate asked three young women whom she previously knew about their experiences on Southland Beach:

> RESEARCHER: It sounds like when you go to the beach alone, you all take certain things into consideration. . . .
>
> c.: Oh, definitely, you plan exactly where you are going to be. . . .
>
> RESEARCHER: What is the consideration? Is it simply the unpleasantness of having someone come up and bothering you?
>
> B. and S.: Unhuh, yea.
>
> B.: It's not so much danger. . . .
>
> c.: I never think of being attacked really, but that might be way back in your subconscious.
>
> s.: Well, maybe it's, in a sense, sort of like a rape, where you have got your little area here and you're protected and if somebody breaks that barrier, he's in a sense sort of raping your territory.
>
> B.: I don't want to be bothered. It's really irritating to have someone approaching you.
>
> s.: That's how I feel. The minute that he's within like reaching distance, all the way around, I feel very uncomfortable, like he is intruding in my area.

When 115 college students were asked whether they would feel that their privacy had been invaded if a stranger sat on their towel, 78 agreed "strongly" that they would, 22 agreed "somewhat," and only 12 disagreed—and these qualified their acceptance of such a stranger by saying that the person would have to be polite, attractive, or otherwise appealing.[2]

Although relatively few incidents that involved such invasions of privacy were observed on Southland Beach, three points stand out. As we noted earlier, most invasions of private space are by small children or dogs. These intrusions almost always take the form of running through another person's territory. The observed reaction to such occurrences is usually slight, although it may involve a dirty look or a yell to be more careful. The next most frequent form of territorial invasion involves men approaching women who are without male escorts. In every case observed except one, the intruding man remained outside the woman's space—that is, approximately three feet beyond her towel—until invited to come closer. The one exception (discussed in Chapter Five) involved a man who lay outside this space but reached into it to touch a girl's ankle. This action evoked an immediately hostile response. The final common form of invasion involves new arrivals to the beach placing their towels too close to the territory of another person or persons. It was not possible to determine what distance was thought to be "too close" in all instances, but as was mentioned in Chapter Five, two of the rule violations that caused people to pick up their towels and leave were of this kind. Interestingly, one was a Chicano family group which moved away because a group of "Anglos" put their towels too close to them.

It is not our purpose here to analyze details of territorial claims and infringements on the beach, as Edney and Jordan-Edney (1974) have done for an East coast beach. We want only to note that beachgoers set up a personal territory on the sand over which they claim exclusive occupancy. Most important, their rights and their interests are bounded by this territory; they feel strongly that they have exclusive occupancy rights within it and they exhibit little interest in what goes on outside of it. This patch of sand is theirs and it is private. As considerable research has pointed out, claiming private territory in this way can be presumed to reduce emotional arousal, decreasing a sense of alarm and vulnerability. Such claims to private territory are said to be most likely to occur in environments that are crowded and competitive

(Mehrabian 1976). What the following woman beachgoer said was repeated by many men and women: "As long as they stay off my blanket they can do anything they want." This view illustrates the way that most beachgoers on Southland Beach feel about their patch of sand.

### Keep to Yourself

As we have already seen, beachgoers typically keep to themselves within the territory they have chosen and marked. They also follow the principle illustrated by the preceding quotation. That is, beachgoers typically avoid paying attention to activities outside of their own territory. For one thing, beachgoers usually avoid direct or prolonged eye contact with outsiders. Even men who look at women typically do so furtively—for example, by pretending to look at something in the distance, or by wearing sunglasses, particularly the mirrored sort that are increasingly popular on this beach. Erving Goffman (1971:46) has noted that it seems to be a rule in our society that "when bodies are naked, glances are clothed." Whether clothed glances at the beach have to do primarily with the state of undress is not entirely clear. For example, in his study of a nude beach in California, Jack Douglas and others (1977) refer to the "studied inattention" of nude beachgoers, while noting that eye contact was made despite the beachgoers' nudity. Indeed, from Douglas' report, it would appear that nude beachgoers are much more willing to look at one another, and to be seen looking at one another, than the conventionally clothed beachgoers at Southland Beach. The avoidance of eye contact on Southland Beach seems to be instead a means of asserting personal privacy, as we shall see. Nevertheless, even people who do look around at the beach, as men are likely to do, attempt to give the appearance that they are paying no attention to the activities of other people.

By the same token, beachgoers take care to avoid any behavior that would invite others to interact with them. Unlike a bar, where as Sherri Cavan (1967:49) has noted, everyone has the right to engage others in conversation and others have an obligation to respond, Southland Beach is a place where people do not expect to have interaction with strangers, and they usually avoid doing anything that may invite it. More than 80 percent of all beachgoers interviewed, male as well as female, said that they avoided any kind of conversation or interaction with persons outside of their own beach territory. Almost all beachgoers said that they generally stay strictly to themselves when they go to the Southland Beach, although a few said that they might respond if spoken to. Only a handful said they usually talked to others if spoken to, and no one said that they usually initiated conversation, although a few said that they sometimes did. This expressed lack of interest in talking to other beachgoers exists even though some older beachgoers freely admit that they are lonely and come to the beach to be around people. However, being *around* other people does not necessarily mean talking to them, especially not initiating a conversation. These comments from beachgoers are typical: "People get along on the beach because they largely do not exist for one another." "Most people who go to the beach get along because they're only there in a partial way. It's like going to the movies. Nobody has anything to do with anybody else." A 31-year-old woman said, "Because people don't communicate, there's no trouble." An older woman added: "It's a big beach and everyone minds their own business within the confines of their own standards." An elderly man made an even stronger statement, but one that was repeated by many other beachgoers: "Everybody minds their own business—wars could be settled on the beach."

Beachgoers often establish their privacy, and their inaccessibility, by immediately burying themselves in a book, or turning on their stomachs to sleep. What is more, both male and female beachgoers say that they do so with the explicit intent of claiming privacy. For example, a 37-year-old man said: "Whenever I go to the beach, the first thing I do is open a book and start to read it. Somehow that makes me feel that I have a right to be there in that particular part of the beach. It makes it my own world, I guess."

Our observations confirm what these beachgoers said. Except for a polite request for the time, beachgoers are unlikely to make any direct approach to one another. It is even rare for them to nod hello to strangers as they approach the beach or leave it. For example, for 60 hours during 1976, special attention was paid to recording any interaction occurring between strangers (that is, persons who did not come to the beach together). Over 6000 beachgoers were observed all over Southland Beach during these 60 hours, and only 24 instances of interaction between strangers were observed. Of these, eight involved distant or fleeting greetings (waving or saying hello to someone who was recognized), four were pick-up attempts, three were requests for the time of day, three more were requests for a cigarette or a match. One person was seen panhandling; one teenager asked another where he could rent a water mattress; one man asked a woman to play backgammon; and on one most unusual occasion an older man and woman who seemed to be strangers engaged in a pleasant chat for 15 minutes or so. It seems obvious from this record that during crowded summer beach conditions, interaction between strangers is infrequent and

Sand sculpture, unattended.

confined almost exclusively to impersonal greetings or requests. It should be noted that this pattern of minimal contact between strangers does not apply to all beaches. For example, there is frequent interaction on County Beach, where many people who come to the beach alone nevertheless know one another. These beachgoers often converse, and may play volleyball or cards together. Interaction is also common on the nude beach that Douglas (1977) described. But on Southland Beach, such interaction is a rarity.

An occasional beachgoer complained to us about this lack of personal interaction. For example, a 28-year-old married woman visiting Southland Beach from the Midwest said this: "People here are rude. They stick to themselves and avoid you. They could care less about meeting other people." A man of 29 who is a regular beachgoer added: "Despite the fun image of the beach, I think that for most people it is largely a sort of deadness in behavior and avoidance of participation. Everyone is hiding in a shell." Another man said: "The beach isn't a social gathering; it happens to be very private." A young woman provided an apt analogy: "It's like being in an elevator where nobody talks." Beachgoers universally agree that the beach is indeed a private place where people stay to themselves in private space with private thoughts. Those few people who would prefer it to be otherwise are a small minority. Almost all beachgoers seem to approve of the personal encapsulation and privacy they find at the beach. This 58-year-old man speaks for the majority opinion: "You can be among many people here and still have privacy. We all prefer it that way."

### Mind Your Own Business

Beachgoers put into action their often-expressed belief that people at Southland Beach should relax and enjoy themselves while allowing others "to do their own thing." As one man put it, "If you don't like what other people are doing, you shouldn't be here. People like that should stay home." In some urban settings, there is no comparable sense of trust or tolerance. On walking along dark streets, or while driving in heavy traffic, people watch carefully the actions of others, and are ready to take alarm at any provocation. For example, users of a British public bathroom were observed to be alert for any sign of impropriety by a stranger, and any unusual behavior readily caused them to be alarmed (Cornwell 1973).[3]

Joan Emerson (1970) has noted that people in public places who are confronted with rule violations often act as if "nothing unusual is happening." This is true at Southland Beach, but even beyond this principle, many beachgoers also act as if behavior which is in no way ambiguous, but is instead manifestly unusual or even troublesome, is nevertheless no concern of theirs. As the police officer quoted in Chapter Four said, people "tune out" one another and become oblivious to the behavior of others.

To be sure, many rule violations at the beach, as elsewhere, are ambiguous enough that it is difficult for a bystander to know what to make of them. Thus we sometimes observed episodes in which it was not easy to determine whether the persons involved were playing or were serious. It is often not difficult, then, for beachgoers, particularly novice beachgoers, to regard much of what happens at the beach as normal, natural beach activity of no danger to anyone. But even if the activity is clearly not usual, not normal, and not play, as in the case of a fistfight between two men, beachgoers typically act as if the matter were none of their affair. They do not intervene, nor do they usually let the activity disrupt their enjoyment of the beach. As one male beachgoer put it, "I've seen some really weird things at the beach, like this dude who was going around nude, or another guy who was punching out his old lady—really slapping her around—but I always figure, like, that's their trip, it's got nothing to do with me." The belief that "nothing really bad could happen at the beach" seems to be translated directly into beach behavior. What happens outside of one's territory is often not noticed at all; if it is noticed, as we saw in the last chapter, it is not usually taken to be problematic or potentially serious; and even when it is seen as being potentially serious, it is generally ignored nevertheless.

In our two summers of beach observations we saw no instance of bystander intervention in which one beachgoer helped another beachgoer who was a stranger. Although this is an impressive record of nonintervention, it could be argued that since we saw nothing serious—such as violations involving theft, violence, or sexual assault—there was no compelling reason for a beachgoer to come to the aid of a stranger, and therefore there was little likelihood that bystanders would intervene. Because this might be a legitimate point, we asked beachgoers, lifeguards, and police officers to recall incidents of theft, violence, or sexual assault which they had actually witnessed from start to finish. In this way we collected 36 episodes of theft of various kinds; bystanders were said to have intervened in only two of these. In one, two youths joined another young man in pursuing a young thief who had stolen his wallet. In the other, a man used a phone to call the police when he saw a woman's purse snatched away from her on the promenade. By the same procedure, we assembled 41 cases of violence between beachgoers. Again, there were only two instances of reported bystander intervention. In the first of these a man who was arguing with a young woman punched her savagely in the nose, leaving her bleeding and dazed. Two men pursued the assailant, but in the opinion of the witness who told the story, they took care to stay far enough behind him that no capture or confrontation could possibly have taken place. This incident raises a significant consideration, which the second instance of intervention bears out. It can be dangerous to intervene. Lifeguards and police officers alike tell tales of the danger of stepping into a violent altercation. Unarmed lifeguards usually avoid it, as we have seen. The police, who do not want to inhibit citizens from preventing crime, nevertheless agree—at least off the record—that for an unarmed and untrained civilian to step into a physical fray can be extremely dangerous.

The second case available to us of bystander intervention at the beach involving violence underscores this point. It was reported by a lifeguard:

An ex-lightweight champion of the world down here on the beach was having some problems with his kid. His kid was running away from a fight. . . . This guy was booting his kid in the fanny because his kid was running from a fight with another kid, and this other guy, a younger man, saw this happening so he went over there and said, 'Don't boot the kid like that.' And the father said, 'Man, don't tell me how to treat my kid, man.' And so he booted the kid again and the other guy said, 'Hey man!' So the next thing I know this boxer jumped all over this other guy and hit him three or four times, a few good shots. He had a pop-top on his finger and cut this guy, lacerated him and opened him up badly. I was standing right here in head-quarters with my eyes wide open like this, and I had to go down and jump in the middle of it. When I got there the boxer kept saying, 'No punk jumps in my face because, man, I'll rub him out.' The police arrested the guy for assault; for using his fists, which were a deadly weapon since he was a boxer.

The point that intervention is dangerous is reinforced by the comments of a regular beachgoer who is himself a black-belt in karate, and a former professional boxer. He says that he never intervenes in other people's troubles on the beach, "Because it is none of my business, and besides you can never tell who has a knife or a gun, even on the beach."

In more than 100 cases of serious sexual affront to a woman beachgoer that we collected, there was not one single instance of direct intervention by another beachgoer. No one walked up to the offending man and said "get lost buddy," and no one attacked or even tried to detain a man who was molesting a woman. Bystanders at the beach do indeed mind their own business, so much so that a woman can scream or struggle against a male assailant while nearby bystanders apparently see, or at least *do*, nothing. Lifeguards may sometimes intervene, often at some risk, as we have seen. The police also intervene, of course, and with their superior training and weaponry they are usually effective. But beachgoers do not intervene. In fact, it is rare that they even take any initiative in calling a lifeguard or a police officer. The one exception to this generalization involves volleyball players who regularly use courts behind tower 16 near the promenade. One woman who frequently sat near these players reported that they twice chased away "creeps" who were annoying her.

We sometimes heard male beachgoers, such as this 30-year-old, talk about experiences in which they *might* have intervened had the offensive behavior gone any farther, but in reality good intentions seem to be as far as matters go:

> Just recently I saw a guy with a camera who was pretending he was a photographer. He approached many women and finally found one who was cooperative. Actually he was scheming. The first four or five women told him to fuck off or they'd stick the camera up his ass, and other like comments. Loud, to notify others. Bluntness, nothing polite. Their responses were almost like a guy in strength. Liberated women. Except for the one he finally cornered; she dug it. He took shots of her from 15 feet away. She noticed and obliged with a smile and a head pose. He immediately approached her. They talked quietly for a few minutes. Friendly. He took other shots and she posed. Nothing gross. Traditional proper woman poses. They talked about 10 minutes more. Finis. Other people were generally (including me) uncomfortable. I'd have been physically aggressive if he'd approached me.
>
> "What if he had continued to photograph unwilling women?"
>
> I'd have stood up and told him to get the fuck off of the area.
>
> "What about your personal safety?"
>
> He was little and appeared feeble. Dobie Gillis type. A woosie.

What is remarkable about this account is not that this man said he might have intervened if the photographer had continued; many men say that they have "thought about" intervening or were even "on the verge" of doing so. Since in fact they do not intervene, we assume that this talk is a kind of bravado, which may be felt sincerely but which is rarely acted out. What is remarkable in this particular instance is the bluntness of the women who were offended. The women we have observed in similar circumstances have rarely made similarly blunt comments. As we shall see in the next chapter, most women who are offended by men are polite, at least initially, and many feel that they should be.

So extreme is bystander apathy on Southland Beach that one of the SCPD detectives responsible for rape investigations insists that there is no safety whatsoever in numbers on the beach, citing as evidence not only rapes that have taken place on the beach "in broad daylight," but a Southland City version of "Kitty Genovese" bystander inaction. On this occasion during the summer of 1975, a young woman left a crowded downtown shopping area at 4 P.M. to retrieve her car from a multi-level parking structure, only to be attacked by a man who beat her with a tire iron. When she played dead, he ran, leaving the woman with sixteen two-inch scalp lacerations, a broken arm, and a broken finger. When this woman staggered out of the parking building—literally covered with blood—she met two different people and pleaded for help. Neither person so much as acknowledged that they had seen her. The victim finally dragged herself into a nearby store, whose owner called the police.

As Latané and Darley (1970) found in their studies of bystanders who do not respond to the distress of others in public places, it may be true that criminals are deterred from violence or other criminal activities by the presence of crowds of people who might serve as witnesses, but if trouble does occur, numbers of people present provide no safety. They conclude (1970:125):

> We have suggested four different reasons why people, once having noticed an emergency, are less likely to go to the aid of the victim when others are present: (1) Others serve as an audience to one's actions, inhibiting him from doing foolish things. (2) Others serve as guides to behavior, and if they are inactive, they will lead the observer to be inactive also. (3) The interactive effect of these two processes will be much greater than either alone; if each bystander sees other bystanders momentarily frozen by

audience inhibition, each may be misled into thinking the situation must not be serious. (4) The presence of other people dilutes the responsibility felt by any single by- stander, making him feel that it is less necessary for him- self to act.

All this fits the behavior of beachgoers on Southland Beach, but we must add that these beachgoers are quite explicit about saying that they come to the beach for fun and not for trouble, and that while they are there it is their intention to mind their own business.

### If Trouble Cannot be Ignored, Move Away

In some urban settings, one cannot easily move away from trouble. In a theater, a ballpark, or a restaurant, one may be forced to sit there and endure affronts and unpleasantries or to take some action against the offending person, because leaving would mean missing the concert or the game or one's dinner. On the beach, as on a public street, one can move away from trouble without loss. Thus, when a beachgoer is so offended or threatened by another person's activity that he can no longer regard it as play or ignore it, his response is likely to be that of picking up his towel and beach gear and simply walking away. As we have seen, it is unusual for an offended beachgoer to remain in his or her territory in order to confront or accuse the offender. We have already recorded several instances of moving away to avoid trouble. In some cases the "offense" was that of nearby teenagers necking too avidly; in others, the beachgoers' territory was invaded by an unwanted stranger. In the majority of such cases, the of- fended beachgoer merely moves a safe distance down the beach, and sets up a new territory. In a few instances, how- ever, the offended person leaves the beach altogether. This latter course seems to be typical for more extreme trouble such as threatened assault or a direct sexual menace, or for the lesser offenses that occur late in the day when the beachgoer may be preparing to leave the beach in any event. Two logically available alternative courses of action are rarely seen: beachgoers do not usually appeal to authorities (the lifeguards or the police) for help, and beachgoers very rarely confront those who offend them.[4]

Because so little serious trouble was observed directly, it was once again necessary to rely on interviews to explore what beachgoers might do when confronted by alarming or annoying situations. Thus in our interviews of 66 women alone on the beach, we asked this hypothetical question: "If something happened that really upset you, what would you do?" Six women said that they simply did not know; five said that they would ignore the trouble and do nothing. Three said they would tell off the troublemaker, while three more said they would yell or scream. The largest number of women—27—would simply pick up their belongings and leave. Two others would run. Another 20 said that they would report the trouble to a lifeguard, and one said she would report it to the police (our beach observations indicate that most women do *not* in fact report offenses to the authorities). The most striking aspect of this response pattern is the reliance of women on indirect action—leaving, running away, or reporting to lifeguards—rather than any kind of direct confrontation. Only three said that they would "tell off" someone who upset them.

Interviews with men yielded the same result. Man after man said that if he were confronted with some really unpleasant situation he would leave rather than "lose his cool." What this man said in response to a question about what he would do if someone were bothering him was typical: "As long as I can get up and leave that's cool; there's no point in making a big deal out of it." The "macho" male who says that he is determined to defend his honor or manhood by a display of pride or aggression does exist on Southland Beach, but he is decidedly in the minority. Most men prefer to walk away from trouble. The exception is men who come to the beach with a wife or girlfriend. These men say they would challenge an offender, and perhaps they would. We have a few accounts in which fights resulted from such confrontations, including a spectacular one in which two women and a man were teasing a young Japanese girl whose frail boyfriend ignored them for awhile. When their taunts grew unbearable he attacked all three using a variety of martial arts; he left them bruised and lacerated, and they left the beach. Such reactions do occur, but we have no way of knowing how many men have "backed down" and walked away when offended in the company of their wife or girlfriend.

With a few exceptions, both men and women say that they insulate themselves against the occurrence of trouble by ignoring it—by minding their own business, or by withdrawing into their own personal space on the beach. When something unpleasant actually occurs, as they admit sometimes happens, they seem to take comfort from their ability simply to walk away from it. As one woman put it, "If you can move away when something bothers you, why cause a ruckus?" These points can be illustrated by what women on the beach said about indecent exposure. First, beachgoers employ the tactic of ignoring it, as illustrated by the comments of an attractive, 43-year-old single woman: "I could care less what others do. I've seen this sort of thing on the beach, but who am I to tell people what to do? I wouldn't report it. I don't pay any attention. It's none of my business. Anyhow, I've seen people nude in movies." Another single woman, also very attractive and somewhat younger, talked about an occasion when a "guy" who was fully clothed sat down next to her and her girlfriend and proceeded forthwith to unzip his pants. The two women simply got up and left. As they left the beach they ran into a police officer and discussed the "flasher" with him, but neither woman wanted to make a complaint. As one of the women said, "It was not that big a deal." A man who was disturbed by the loud obscenities of nearby teenage boys also got up and moved away. "They were really getting to me with their filthy mouths, but there's plenty of beach here. I just left them there to entertain themselves with their adolescent bullshit."

In summary, beachgoers think of the beach as a relaxing and safe place. They establish a territory as their private preserve, neither encouraging nor seeking contacts with strangers. They keep to themselves and mind their own business. If something unpleasant nevertheless occurs, they ignore it, or if necessary move away from its source. People sit or lie in private patches of sand, tolerating, trusting, and ignoring strangers all around them. If they are upset by something, rather than choosing to react, and perhaps making matters worse, they move away. These typical actions are consistent with beliefs that define the beach as safe and pleasant. It seems plausible to conclude that these beliefs and actions serve to (1) reduce the opportunities for conflict among beachgoers, (2) encourage the perception of potentially troubling beach activities as normal and not serious, and (3) restrict the likelihood that a beachgoer's reaction to an offense will cause trouble to become more serious.

To explore these matters further, let us examine the beliefs and behaviors of the most vulnerable of all beachgoers—women who come to the beach without men.

# Women on
# Southland Beach

As we have seen, there are many women on Southland Beach. On an ordinary summer day, in fact, the majority of beachgoers are women. Many of them come to the beach alone; others come with small children, or with other women. Most of them visit this beach year after year. There are many urban places these women avoid if no man is with them—dark streets, poorly lighted parking structures, "tough" neighborhoods, bars. In some places, like dark streets, they fear assault, sexual or otherwise. In other places, like bars, "unaccompanied" women fear they will invite unwanted male attention. A sense of vulnerability is something that women alone in urban settings must learn to live with. Yet lone women not only go to Southland Beach, they do something that would be unthinkable for them in most other public places—they undress.

The paradox continues. We have seen that trouble does occur on this beach and that the victims are often women. Both police officers and lifeguards express concern over the welfare of women, whom they regard as especially vulnerable; in fact, some insist that a woman alone is definitely not safe on Southland Beach. But women themselves do not share this concern. They enjoy the beach, they return to it, and they say that it is safe. For example, a woman in her thirties was indignant when she said: "Of course, it's safe here; I've been coming to this beach since I was a little kid." Yet our research indicates that although most women who come to the beach alone can look forward to a trouble-free day, something unpleasant will happen to a substantial minority of them, and a few will have a downright frightening experience.

The study of the multiple realities of human minds or human situations has received a good deal of psychological and sociological attention, not only in such well-known approaches as those of William James or Alfred Schutz, but in many recent writings as well.[1] There is nothing inherently baffling, then, in the fact that some women construe Southland Beach as a safe and pleasant place, while others see it as a place where women are in peril. What is of interest is *how* women establish and maintain their reality that this beach is safe and pleasant.

### Problems Women Face on Southland Beach

Before asking how it is that lone women manage to make beachgoing a pleasurable experience, we should review the kinds of annoyances and unpleasantries women at the beach must cope with. First, there are the everyday trivialities— thrown balls or frisbees, kicked sand, bee stings, loud radios, litter, and the like. These problems can be annoying, as many women acknowledge; but they are also rather trivial, and lone women are no more vulnerable to them than anyone else. Another problem common to all beachgoers is theft. Yet as we have seen, theft from beachgoers on the sand does not seem to be commonplace, and many women say that they have never really been worried about it. Perhaps this is so because so few women bring anything of value to the beach with them. Perhaps it is simply that theft occurs so infrequently. Lone women probably are more vulnerable to violence than other beachgoers are, but such crimes are not very common either.

A lone woman at area 16.

The most common and potentially troublesome problem faced by lone women on the beach is receiving unwanted attention from men. As we have seen, women who go to this beach (especially South beach) must run a gauntlet of strange and menacing men on the beach fringe. Once on the sand they are available for men to stare at, talk to, expose themselves to, masturbate toward, touch, grab, or even rape. Because men do all of these things to women on this beach, it is intriguing that lone women nevertheless succeed in making beachgoing so pleasurable an experience.

### Avoiding Trouble

Part of the success women have in enjoying the beach appears to result from the care that most of them take to avoid trouble. Women who go to Southland Beach without a man as escort express the same beliefs and engage in the same behaviors described for all beachgoers in the last chapter. But they follow additional routines as well. As we observed the conduct of all kinds of beachgoers, it became apparent that women—especially lone women—almost always followed a predictable routine of beach behavior.

First, they almost always wear some sort of blouse or shirt

over their bathing suit as they approach the beach. The only
exceptions commonly seen were teenaged girls, usually in
groups of two or more. About 75 percent of these lone
women also wear shorts, pants, or a skirt over their bathing
suits as well. Therefore, as these women approach the beach
across parking lots or walkways where strange or menacing
men are most likely to be found, they are modestly attired.
They also walk briskly and purposefully toward the sand.
They do not slow down or meander, and they keep their eyes
strictly to themselves. However blatantly men may stare at
them or make comments, women rarely acknowledge they
have seen or heard anything, but instead keep walking ahead
as if they were both deaf and blind. Men on the sand may
comment as they pass by, or even invite them to join them,
but only two out of 100 women whom we observed closely
were heard to respond, and these two both declined the invi-
tation in a pleasant but firm way as they walked by. Once on
the beach, lone women head directly for an open patch of
sand, which is usually near another woman or a family
group, but is not close to a lone man or a group of men. Once
this spot has been reached, the woman establishes her territory by spreading out her towel and quickly sitting on it.
Some women sit fully clothed for a few minutes, but almost
all undress as far as their bathing suits within two to three
minutes. Between 30 and 40 percent of lone women stand
while they undress; a few of these seductively wiggle out of
their clothing as nearby men watch appreciatively. But the
majority of lone women sit while they undress, presumably
because they recognize that it is more modest and less conspicuous than standing. These women remove their blouses
and pants without any obvious seductiveness. They then
apply suntan lotion and in a minute or two lie down, usually
on their stomachs, and begin to read or to sleep. Ordinarily
they do not sit, which might indicate that they were approachable, nor do they look around except for a glance or
two of orientation. If they do look around, they avoid eye
contact with nearby men. If, as many women do, they undo
the back strap of their bikini tops while lying on their

stomachs, they do so very modestly, taking care that their breasts are not exposed even momentarily, and they seldom unfasten their tops until they have been at the beach for 20 or 30 minutes. If they must leave the sand to visit a bathroom or to buy refreshments, about 70 percent of them put their shirts or blouses (but not pants or skirts) back on before doing so. Almost all walk briskly and avoid eye contact as before.

In addition to the interviews with women which were discussed earlier, we spent many hours interviewing 51 women beachgoers whom we knew as friends or acquaintances.[2] We asked these women about their feelings and actions as beachgoers on Southland Beach, and their answers were detailed and thoughtful. These interviews were unstructured and informal, yet they focused on specific topics: women's reasons for going to the beach, their routines of beach activity, how they avoided trouble there, and what they did if trouble started. One thing that almost all women agreed about is that they are aware of and practice the routines we have just described. Many provided details of their routines, such as the fact that they park as close as possible to the spot of beach they are going to visit so that they can shorten the distance they must walk before reaching the sand, and that they often feign sleep when they first arrive in order to communicate their unavailability to men who may be watching:

> I've been going to the same place on the beach for years [near tower 18] but I'm sort of nervous while I'm parking my car in the lot. I get out of that lot in a big hurry and get out on the sand. The sand is like a sanctuary for me. Once I'm there I relax and mellow out. Usually I lay (sic) down and sleep for a while, or at least I close my eyes. To me it's a way of showing myself how safe and cozy I am, like a little kid in bed who pulls the covers over her head. I think that sleeping also turns off any creeps who might be planning to come over and bug me.

It is clear that women are aware that they are being stared at by countless male eyes as they approach the beach and as they undress. Different women made these typical comments. "You feel that everyone in the world is watching you, like you're on display." "You just want to get on your little towel and lie down so you're not so exposed." "Sometimes you glance around as you're taking your clothes off and all you see are men craning their necks to stare at you." Most women made remarks like this, which emphasize their sense of vulnerability as they walk to the sand and as they undress. Some women were angry about it, but most seemed to accept it as a part of beachgoing. A few, however, admitted that they like being looked at—if the stares aren't too open—and a few also admitted that it is an erotic experience for them to undress in front of so many men. One attractive woman in her thirties, who is a regular and solitary beachgoer, said: "It's not like I'm teasing or coming on to them, it's just that it feels good to know that all those guys are looking at me and appreciating my body. I don't want men to talk to me. It's just the fantasy of it, the wicked woman in me I suppose." Another added that while she did not seek male attention at the beach, she was nevertheless flattered by having her body admired: "It's a compliment when men pick up on you at the beach; everything's hanging out after all."

Whether women like being looked at or not, there can be no doubt that men at the beach like to look. Our observations leave no doubt about this. Most men look at women much of the time on the beach. When we interviewed male beachgoers, friends and strangers alike admitted that looking at women was one of the major attractions of the beach for them. Most men say that they look at all attractive women, but that when a woman is with a man, the looking must be especially covert. Even when the woman is unescorted, the glances are usually still indirect, but many men admit to more open stares at such women from time to time. Men also agree that with rare exceptions, women on the beach will not meet their eyes or acknowledge their attention. They feel that women only rarely give any sign that they are approachable. Women agree that eye contact is the most obvious sign of their availability, saying that if they want to express any availability to a man, they need only make eye contact with him to do so. The same rule applies on the nude beach

A man spent the day here, watching women.

studied by Douglas and others (1977:174); even when the woman is nude, eye contact is a powerful signal of availability. Perhaps the only more inviting sign on either beach is a warm smile.

The views of the following man, who described himself as a dedicated "beach hustler," tell us something about a man's point of view about women on the beach, and about the coping skills of women as well. This man is a handsome, athletic sort in his late thirties whose profession allows him several afternoons a week at the beach to play volleyball—, and to pick up women:

Well, I've been playing volleyball here since I was in college and, you know, this *is* where the girls are. I mean there are some of the most gorgeous girls in the world here. It's fantastic . . . sometimes I just can't believe it. It's hard to tell when a girl is going to pick up on you, I mean except for those that are really gross, really brazen. Some do their numbers like losing a bikini strap, or walking down to the water real sexy, swiveling their butts. You know. Then there are the volleyball groupies who just hang around all the time. Some of them are really aggressive. Bad news. But most women are just there on their towels soaking up the rays and you can't tell whether you're going to score or not. If they're reading or writing letters it's pretty good because it gives you an opening, a conversation piece, like, "So you like Saul Bellow, too!" or "The way you're writing you're going to get rich!" But if they're just lying there it's more difficult because it's hard to approach a girl who's lying down without scaring her a little. If the girl is on her belly and has her top undone, you leave them alone. They're very jumpy in that situation. . . . What you do is decide on your opening— something that fits the girl and won't sound trite, then you move up. You don't stand there, that only scares them. You kneel down or squat down, not too close, and say something cool, like about her book, or has she seen this play, or whatever. If she sits up and talks back, she's interested. If she rolls over on her belly or just gives you "yesses" and "no's," you're in trouble. Some girls will just shine you on for a while and then freeze you out, but you can usually tell. Whatever your approach is, you don't come on strong, you act friendly and cool and sophisticated. I usually ask them if they play volleyball, mostly to let them know what I'm all about. But it's not like a bar where you know any single girl is available if the right man comes along. At the beach, girls are unpredictable. They aren't sure about you and they aren't sure they want to have anything to do with you, but they aren't sure they don't either, so they play along for awhile. Some are really cold. They're sick of men hassling them and you just can't win with them, but most girls are cool and polite and it depends on you. You take a chance, but I love it because I only go after the blue-chip lovelies, so what can I lose? . . . I do pretty well. I get some dates, and when I get a date I always score. I mean *always*. It's not my fatal charm, it's my boat. My big line at the beach is "Would you like to go for a sail in my boat some-day?" [He has a trimaran.] A beach girl can't resist that. They almost always perk up when I invite them to go sail-ing. Sometimes I ask them to dinner first, then to go sailing the next day. I sometimes tell them after dinner that my boat is right there in the Marina and how would they like to look at it. Sometimes we just go sailing first and let things happen afterwards. Either way, we wind up in my apartment at the Marina where all you can see is boats and ocean. I do all right."

Most of the women we talked to thought that their efforts to avoid male attention were effective, but in saying this they revealed something that complicates matters. Many women who go to the beach alone do not want to avoid *all* men. Lone women of all ages admit that one of the primary attractions of the beach is the presence of handsome men in bathing suits. Most of these single women admit further that should a really handsome and interesting man approach them, they would not mind talking to him. "I'm always open if Mr. Right comes along—Robert Redford, for example."

Almost all of the 66 lone women we interviewed on South-land Beach said that men at the beach should not be encour-aged because they are only interested in "pick-ups." Yet 22 of these 66 women said that they *had* made friends with a man at the beach. To explore further the willingness of women to talk to strangers, we asked if they were often approached by men who were strangers to them. Forty-five of the 66 women said that they were. We then asked how they felt about this, and learned that 33 of the women thought it was all right as long as the men were not offensive. Of the 51 women friends and acquaintances whom we interviewed at length, 34 said that they were frequently approached by strange men; 24 of them felt that this was all right if the man were particularly interesting or attractive to them. A few, especially younger single women, were downright enthusiastic. One attractive 34-year-old single woman said mournfully, "Unfortunately, no one ever bothers me." Even a 35-year-old married woman, who happened to be unusually attractive, exulted in the fact that one day a police helicopter landed near her on the beach and the officer came over to her saying that she looked so great from the air he just had to see her up close. Nine of the 66 women strongly objected to male attention. Surprisingly, all nine were single, eight of them being under 35 years old. For example, one very pretty young woman, who was virtually topless on the beach when we spoke to her, said flatly, "I don't come to the beach to meet men." Three additional women were not certain, saying such things as "If it's a nice-looking guy I'd be interested." Seventeen of these 51 women we interviewed at length objected to any approach by a strange man, with nine of them objecting strongly. Our beach observations indicate that women alone on this beach rarely initiate such encounters, but they are not entirely closed to them with the "right" man.

We saw many instances in which men of all ages and appearances were seen moving up and down the beach attempting to strike up conversations with unescorted women. If the man was old, bizarre, bedraggled, or abusive, he was rejected rather quickly, sometimes even rudely. In one such instance, a dirty and dishevelled man approached a trio of young women and asked for a date that night. One girl declined quite coldly. When he then berated her, the other two women joined the first in telling him to "get lost." However, we have also seen attractive young men receive a warm welcome from women. In several instances these men succeeded in making dates, and three actually left the beach with the woman they "picked up."

One attractive young woman summarized matters this way: "When someone comes and intrudes on your little territory at the beach, you are definitely on the defensive. But then again, there may be mitigating circumstances. Like this may be someone who is physically attractive and you're going to deal with this man in a totally different way than someone who is unattractive. . . . If they are attractive, I may not care to really talk to them, but I won't be rude. I may not encourage the conversation, but I'll have a whole different mode of talking."

### When Men Approach Women

Our observations confirm that when a lone woman is approached by a strange man who is attractive to her, her reaction will usually be cool but not totally rejecting. Indeed, most women said that they felt an obligation to be polite as long as the man was not offensive. As one attractive young woman said, "Women are taught to be polite in this society. You can't just say 'fuck off' to any guy you don't like." Men who ask for a match, or the time, or to discuss a book are not immediately offensive; trite, perhaps, but not offensive. Those who launch directly into sexually loaded topics are.

On the nude beach described by Douglas and others (1977:172), the ambience is said to be frankly sexual. Thus men who approach women—"vultures" as they are called—may be successful by the use of a direct sexual conversation, and some women respond in kind. But while there is an undeniably erotic undertone at Southland Beach, a direct approach to sexuality is not considered appropriate. The following story from a 22-year-old occasional beachgoer is characteristic of the problems some single women face on Southland Beach:

> One day I went to the beach and I really didn't want to talk to anybody. I wanted to be by myself, and on this

particular day I had three different people come up to me. One of them was an old man, an old, pale, white, wrinkled man. He came up to me and stood over me and said, "Oh, you have a nice body." Well I don't know how he could say that, I had my clothes on, it was cold . . . but anyway, I didn't reply. He asked, "Do you mind if I sit down here?" I said, "Well, suit yourself, but I'm going to go to sleep." So he sat down and talked about, I don't know . . . he had a straw hat on. And he tried to make some sort of conversation. When I don't feel like talking to someone, I'll answer with just a yes or no, won't encourage any conversation. And after awhile he said "Would you like to have dinner with me tonight?" I said, "I don't think so." At the time I had a gold ring on and he looked at it, and fortunately it had turned so it looked like a wedding band, and he asked if I were married and I said "Yes! Yes! I'm married and my husband would *not* go along with this." So he got up and walked off to bother someone else, I imagine. Then a few minutes later, this other guy came by and told me how he liked to come to the beach and talk to girls about sex, and weird things like that, and I rolled over on my stomach, because when I'm lying on my back I feel particularly vulnerable. At first he seemed friendly and I didn't think he was too bad, but when he started bringing this into the conversation I thought, "Oh no, no, I'm not going to have anything to do with you." So he finally left. There was one other who walked by and just said "Hello," or something like that, and I didn't reply. About this time I decided I'd had it for the day.

This comment by a very pretty 27-year-old married woman, who was reading *Fear of Flying* on the beach when interviewed, is also typical: "I was bothered all day yesterday by guys trying to pick me up. I guess it was because I didn't have my daughter with me. I didn't like being bothered that way, but I've never really thought of being afraid at the beach."

Another woman, 28 years old, was on the beach with her small son and his playmate when an attractive young man approached her quite closely and asked, "Are you still married?" She was taken aback by his bold opening line, but was quickly disarmed when he said that she had looked so sweet lying there with her eyes closed that he had been tempted to kiss her. She said that the "girlish, flirtatious part of her" was touched, but when she discovered after some further conversation that he was not especially bright or interesting to her she began to answer his questions as briefly as possible, and he soon got up and walked away, leaving a business card with her. Encounters like these were reported by about two-thirds of all the women we interviewed.

Women consistently say that they are able to terminate unwanted encounters whenever they wish without much unpleasantness. Some women, including older married ones, say that they enjoy feeling that they are desirable to men, and that the possibility of male attention at the beach is pleasantly titillating, not menacing. Ten of the 66 women interviewed on the beach reported that they met a man there with whom they later had a memorable sexual encounter or romantic relationship. There are many days when women do not feel like being approached, and some of the men who approach them would be objectionable on any day, but most of the time women feel they can control their situation. The following remark is typical in its confidence: "Once in a while a guy comes by who interests me and I'll talk to him. Most of the time I really don't want to be bothered, though, so I'm very cold to them and they get the message."

### Men Who Make Trouble

However confident women may feel that men will get the message, some men don't, and others have a message of their own that they are determined to deliver. It is not surprising then that about one-third of all women interviewed reported having a seriously unpleasant encounter with a man. As one young woman said: "The beach is such a permissible set of circumstances. You're physically so exposed. People that are walking down the street are generally caught up in their own little world, and people don't stop you because you seem to be going somewhere. But you're in a stationary position at the beach, you're just lying there by yourself and you're much more vulnerable to someone accosting you."

To examine further this sense of vulnerability, we posed a series of hypothetical questions to women who were alone on Southland Beach. We first asked them what they would do if something were stolen from them while they were on the beach. Twenty-two of the 66 women said that they would report it; five did not know where they could report it, three mentioned the police, and 14 mentioned the lifeguards. Two women said they would chase the thief, with one of these, a teenager, adding that she had once done so. Four women said that they would scream or become angry, while 16 others said that they would simply forget the loss and do nothing. Another 21 women said that they did not know what they would do, that they had actually never thought about theft on the beach; they added that they were not worried about such a thing happening.

When we asked a question about a more commonplace happening, however, the women were sure what they would do. We asked what they would do if they or someone with them needed first aid. Only five did not know. Two others said they knew enough first aid to treat themselves, and all the rest said that they would go to a lifeguard. Quite a few said that they had in fact taken some sort of injury to a lifeguard in the past. Having resolved that women on the beach knew what they would do in regard to at least one kind of trouble, we then asked, "What would you do if you saw a man exposing himself?" We assumed that this behavior was fairly common on the beach and would be upsetting to women who witnessed it. We were surprised to discover that 37 women said that they would simply ignore such behavior, unless, as one woman put it, "He did it right in my face." Most added that they would not be upset by such conduct, and quite a few commented that nudity did not bother them at all. A few said with apparent sincerity that if the man were good-looking they would watch and enjoy the performance. Two women did not know what they would do, and the remaining 27 said that they would take some sort of action.

Two would yell at the man; one, a teenaged girl, said she had once done so, shouting "Hey man, you're sick." Eleven women would get up and leave; twelve would report the occurrence to a lifeguard, and two would call the police. Some of these women expressed their indignation about "flashers" or "perverts," and several added that they had themselves seen such behavior and reported it. Nevertheless, the majority said that they would do nothing if they saw it, and many of these women had in fact witnessed indecent exposure and done nothing about it. There were no differences in age or marital status between women who objected to "flashers" and those who did not. What is more, women who were alone on the beach were just as accepting as women who came with other women. Surprisingly, so were women who came with their children. One of these quite seriously said, "If the guy were good-looking, I'd take my kids away and then come back and watch him." Another said, while her seven-year-old daughter was listening, that she would simply sit and watch. In all, only 14 of the 66 women said that they would "report" indecent exposure, and women actually report such behavior even less frequently than they say they would.

While most women appear to be remarkably unflappable by at least some kinds of sexual affronts, men *do* accost women at Southland Beach, and some of these men cannot always be ignored or disregarded. Thus, some men blithely stay on, continuing their line of conversation despite the woman's refusal to talk to them and her requests that they leave. In fact, some stay and talk even though the woman has gone to sleep (or has pretended to). Some of these men talk in outrageously obscene terms, often asking women to engage in sexual relations with them, but sometimes merely chatting in a salaciously offensive way. Others may expose themselves; while this often happens at a distance, it is sometimes the case that a man who sits or stands close to a lone woman will expose himself to her. Some of these men masturbate. Other men touch women, sometimes softly caressing an arm or an ankle, but other times making a sudden, violent grab at a more intimate target. Once in a while, a man hurls himself onto a woman, kissing and fondling her or tearing off her bathing suit. Rape, too, is attempted on the sand in the daylight.

As we have seen, about one-third of the women we interviewed said that they have never been accosted in any of these offensive ways. But an equal number acknowledged that they have been, often more than once, sometimes referring angrily to the "creeps" and "weirdos" who won't leave them alone. We collected a corpus of over 100 episodes of this kind from lone women, other beachgoers, lifeguards, police, and direct observation. From these episodes it seems clear that women have developed routines for avoiding male attention, and for terminating ordinary approaches should they prove to be unwanted, just as they have learned to ignore men who expose themselves from a reasonable distance. But their defenses against physical intrusion into their private territory or against direct sexual advances are by no means predictable, nor are they always effective.

If, for example, a man simply ignores the woman's cold shoulder treatment and continues to sit close to her and talk, the woman may try to sleep (always on her stomach, never on her back), or she may tell him to leave, or she may herself get up and leave. Women report doing all these things, and we have seen them done. Some women who are upset actually go home, but most merely move to another spot on the beach. However, when the man makes a physical advance, the woman's reaction is in no sense calculated.

For example, a nice-looking young man was seen by two lifeguards to crawl up to an attractive young woman who was lying on her back alone on the sand. When he reached her, he leaned over her—and vomited on her stomach. She awoke in a panic, but when the lifeguards rushed up she refused to make a formal complaint, saying that she was a psychology major and "understood." Later, the same man repeated this sequence, and this time his victim ran from the beach before the lifeguards could talk to her.

A woman in her thirties recalled being asleep on her stomach on a crowded Sunday afternoon when a fully dressed young man sat down beside her. Without a word, he unzipped his pants and began to masturbate. With great sangfroid, she put her head down and pretended to sleep. She said that she was prepared to scream or run if he touched her, but he didn't and when she looked up in 10 minutes or so, he was gone. Another young woman, in her twenties, was also lying on her stomach reading a book around noon on a crowded summer day. Another fully dressed young man sat down next to her, saying something about how pretty she looked. She refused to reply, but before she could turn away from him to her book she saw him begin to undo his pants. She tried to ignore him, but the temptation to glance at him to see what he was doing was too great. When she looked, she saw that he had pulled his pants all the way down to his knees and was masturbating while kneeling only a foot or two away from her. She said, "Hey man, I'm really not into this" and stood up to leave. He responded in a calm, conversational tone: "Will you be coming right back?" The woman, who rushed away from the beach in disorder, was speechless.

Many women report that a man whom they found unattractive, and were trying to ignore, reached out and fondled them in a sexual way. Their reactions varied from silent indignation, to a harsh verbal report, to flight. Other women have been subjected to more objectionable sexual advances. One teenaged girl reported that a handsome young man approached her in the water and ripped off her bikini before grabbing and fondling her "all over." She finally broke away and ran crying to a lifeguard tower. Another woman, in her early forties, was sitting on her towel on a crowded summer day when a man in bathing trunks suddenly sat down beside her, slipped his hand inside her bikini top and kissed her neck. She struggled away, managed to yell "hey," and watched in astonishment as the man got up and casually walked away. Other women have fought, screamed, and fled from similar assaults. Some reported the assault, most did not. One 22-year-old woman was lying alone on the sand on a crowded Sunday afternoon when a young man, who was fully dressed, lay down beside her and tried to pull her into his embrace. He said to her, as if to justify his behavior, "I haven't had a good fuck for two or three years." She struggled away, ran off the beach, and used a pay phone to call the lifeguards, who in turn called the police. Another attractive woman was assaulted in a similar way; she also fled the beach, and as she reached her car in the parking lot she saw a police patrol car. She did not report the incident, later saying to us, "It wasn't that big a deal."

Some women reflect upon these encounters with humor and bravado, recalling what they should have said, or would say the next time. "I'd laugh and say that's the smallest one I've ever seen." "I'd just back off and hit him in the balls." But in actuality, words fail women who are victimized in these ways. They rarely say anything that is devastating. They are most likely to say something inane such as "Hey" or "Stop" or "What do you think you're doing?" They do not deliver well-placed kicks or karate chops either. They struggle away and run. Assaults of this kind, it would seem, are impossible to prepare for. Apparently, few women are prepared either for the time or the embarrassment that they believe a police report would entail, since they commonly say that reporting a sexual assault to the police is "one endless hassle" and that "nothing would come of it anyhow."

In the face of all this evidence that women are vulnerable to trouble on this beach, one fact stands out. The majority of women we spoke to, either on Southland Beach, or in their own homes, said that nothing "really unpleasant" had ever happened to them there. This may be an accurate reflection of the low incidence of trouble on the beach, but this majority view that "really serious" trouble is rare on Southland Beach may come, at least in part, from women's conviction that nothing serious *could* happen at the beach. As a result, even women who have been grabbed or fondled are able to conclude that the attack was not really serious.

### Nothing Serious Could Happen at the Beach

The women we interviewed on the beach, or elsewhere, insisted that Southland Beach was perfectly safe. As a 28-year-old married woman said, "I wouldn't be coming to this beach if there were any really serious trouble here." Another woman, this one in her thirties, put it this way: "I have been coming to this beach since I was a teenager. I've never seen any real trouble here. Everybody comes here to have fun and people just get along with each other. There's room for people to spread out and if someone is bothering you, you can always get up and move. There's no reason to be afraid. Fear breeds fear, so I'm not going to believe that there's any danger at the beach. My God, if I believed that, I wouldn't feel safe anywhere anymore. If I can't be safe at the beach, where can I feel safe?" These views are typical. Women go to Southland Beach alone feeling happy and content, confident that nothing really unpleasant will occur to them. The women we interviewed on the beach had been going there for an average of 13 years. They had achieved their sense of security and well-being in spite of their apprehension about the strange-looking men whom they must sometimes pass in order to reach the sand, and in spite of the various kinds of men who sometimes approach them. Fully one-third of these women continue to regard this beach as both pleasant and safe, and they return there, often to the same place where they had the unpleasant encounter. The past encounters, they said, were "nothing serious."

### Conclusion

It seems undeniable that women who go to Southland Beach successfully define this beach for themselves as a safe and pleasant place. Of all the women we interviewed at this beach or elsewhere, no more than a handful expressed any serious concern about potential danger there. We believe that this definition of Southland Beach as safe and pleasant is a product of several complex factors. First, it seems likely, although we have little evidence, that female beachgoers have grown up with a definition of "the beach" as both safe and pleasant. Films, television, and novels reinforce this conception. Newspapers seldom report crimes or disturbances on the beach, and even the recent film "Lifeguard," which did portray trouble on the beach, including "flashers," made light of trouble, showing clearly that the lifeguards had these matters well in hand, and that women were in no real danger. Instead of problems, the film emphasized romance.

Furthermore, most of the Anglo women at Southland Beach have been going there since their high school days, and many spoke nostalgically about the wonderful beach experiences of those years. We also assume, again on the basis of indirect evidence, that all these women are highly motivated to enjoy the beach. They drive great distances, pay to park, put up with various indignities—and most of them come back to the beach as often as they possibly can. Like other beachgoers they establish their own private territory, keep to themselves, mind their own business, and if trouble cannot be ignored, they move away. In addition, it seems likely that most of these women have in fact developed coping skills that permit them to avoid the uninvited male attention to which they are vulnerable. These skills seem to serve women well in terms of the stares, comments, or approaches of most men on the beach. Women feel in control, and as far as we can determine, they usually are. Recall that one-third of these unescorted women beachgoers (many of whom were strikingly attractive) reported that *nothing* bothers them at the beach. Finally, the kinds of trouble that women cannot control—mainly the direct advances of offensive men—are relatively infrequent. A woman can go to the beach many times without becoming the victim of an overt sexual affront.

Many women beachgoers are quite literally disbelieving when they are told about the kinds of "broad daylight" sexual offenses that come to the attention of the lifeguards or the police. They simply do not believe that such things could occur "with all those people around." Other women who have experienced an unpleasant encounter with a man—

being accosted or molested in an offensive and menacing way—nevertheless say that these episodes, while nasty, are "no big deal" because, after all, one is always able to walk away and leave if necessary. They add with great assurance that given the daylight and the presence of fellow beachgoers they are secure against any serious harm. This is their reality, and they are sure of it.

# 10

## Conclusion

Southland Beach, California, has become one of this country's most urban beaches. It is readily accessible to one of the largest and most heterogeneous urban populations in the United States, and these diverse peoples visit it by the millions each year. We have asked how it is possible for so many strangers of all ages, ethnic groups, and income levels to visit this strip of sand, remove almost all their clothing, often drink alcohol, smoke marijuana, and take other drugs, and yet manage not only to avoid conflict with one another but to enjoy themselves thoroughly.

What we have seen and heard from these beachgoers leaves no doubt that they do enjoy themselves. We have also seen that there can be trouble among them, yet during the peak crowding hours of 10 A.M. to 4 P.M. during the summer, trouble on Southland Beach is relatively infrequent and inconsequential. We have concluded that the overwhelming majority of beachgoers can confidently expect to have a pleasant and trouble-free day when they visit this beach.

How readers will feel about the beach dangers we have described is difficult to anticipate. One reader might conclude that the three aggravated assaults we reported, which took place during the most crowded part of the day over a 90-day period of summer 1975, constitute clear evidence of danger. But another might point out that there were over six million people at the beach during that period, meaning that the probability that any individual would have become a victim of aggravated assault was less than one in two million. It might also be pointed out that during 1975 there were 205 aggravated assaults and many more less serious assaults reported in Southland City—a place with only 90,000 residents. Rape provides another illustration. In both 1974 and 1975 there were two reported rapes on Southland Beach during the day. One person might recoil in horror at the thought that rape could occur on the beach at all during the day, but another might prefer to note that only two rapes occurred despite the presence at the beach of between 12 and 16 million people each year. There were 51 rapes in 1974 and 48 in 1975 among Southland City's 90,000 residents. Another person might favorably compare the dangers of beachgoing with those of driving one's car in the same area. For example, in 1975, along the one and a half mile portion of the six-lane highway that parallels the northern part of Southland Beach, there were 36 accidents with 54 injuries, many of which were serious.

The violence we have seen at the beach seldom troubles ordinary beachgoers. Thus we know of no parallel, on the sandy part of Southland Beach, for the daytime violence both commonly and casually reported elsewhere in the city.[1] For example, consider this matter-of-fact report from a nearby automobile raceway:

An argument over spilled beer at the Irwindale Raceway led to the stabbing death of a 20-year-old La Habra man, sheriff's deputies said. Kent A. Pruitt was walking to a refreshment stand when he accidentally kicked over another man's beer, witnesses said. They said Pruitt apologized and bought the man another beer, but the man started an argument. Deputies said Pruitt was stabbed three times with a six-inch switchblade knife. He was pronounced dead at Santa Teresita Hospital. His assailant, who fled with a girlfriend, was described as about 20 years old, 5 feet 9 inches tall, with long curly black hair and a Fu Manchu moustache. (*Los Angeles Times*, March 8, 1976.)

Although comparable research is lacking, we also doubt that gang violence at Southland Beach has ever reached the proportions often reported from rock concerts. For example, this was recently reported from a Detroit rock concert:

Detroit (UPI)—Gangs of black youths terrorized rock concert fans in downtown Detroit, forcing their way into an evening concert at Cobo Hall and beating and robbing members of the audience.

The violence then spread outside, where at least one woman was raped on a sidewalk, several other people were assaulted and robbed, and two stores were broken into, police said Monday.

At least 21 youths, six of them juveniles, were arrested and jailed on charges ranging from larceny to armed robbery. (*Los Angeles Times*, August 17, 1976.)

Considering the conditions at Southland Beach that could encourage conflict, it seems reasonable to conclude that remarkably little serious trouble occurs. The beach is not quite as idyllic as most beachgoers believe it to be, but by current standards of urban life, a summer day at Southland Beach can be expected to be a safe and pleasant experience. We must now ask why that is so. In doing so, we must first dismiss the assertion that it is simply "natural" for so many different kinds of people to get along together under the conditions present at Southland Beach. Instead, it seems likely that this beach is transformed from a potentially dangerous place into one that is relatively safe and pleasant by the interrelated effects of (1) lifeguard and police protection, (2) beachgoers' definitions of the beach situation, and (3) beachgoers' routines of behavior.

### Social Control by Lifeguards and Police

As we have seen, the combined activities of lifeguards and police officers play a part in preventing trouble and reducing its seriousness. Part of their success is due to the presence of lifeguards in towers along the shoreline; this presence almost certainly deters some criminal activity, and the direct intervention of lifeguards in other potentially dangerous or criminal actions must also serve to limit the occurrence of trouble on the sand. Yet the lifeguards are primarily concerned with what goes on in the water, not on the sand, so their police role is a limited one at best. However, they do often use their telephones to call the police when trouble occurs. Rapid police response to such calls, combined with their routine patrol activities, must also contribute to the control of trouble on this beach.

It is always possible to argue, as some beachgoers and a few lifeguards have done, that police presence on the beach creates problems that would otherwise not exist. However, aside from an occasional act of hostility toward the police, as when young people "oink" or otherwise taunt the officer in Unit 99, or on rare occasions when a young beachgoer throws a ball or sand at the police vehicle, direct evidence for this assertion is confined to those instances when police enforcement of municipal ordinances offends some beachgoers. The ordinance against dogs is an example, but even here it should be recalled that while some beachgoers want to bring their dogs to the beach, a good many others are bothered by dogs on the sand and complain about them. In any event, police officers on Southland Beach do not spend a great deal of their time enforcing minor municipal ordinances. Most of their time is spent in responding to citizen complaints; the remaining time is spent in patrol, which may or may not involve enforcing ordinances against dogs, alcohol, or barbeques. It seems reasonable to conclude that the primary effect of their presence on the beach is *not* that of creating trouble which would otherwise not occur.

On the contrary, there is reason to suppose that police presence on Southland Beach is a significant deterrent to certain kinds of trouble. This deterrent may operate in several ways. First, police presence on the beach may serve as a visual deterrent. How effective this role may be is difficult to assess. We do know that many beachgoers say that they have never seen Unit 99 or any other police officer on the beach, but others have seen the police and say that they feel secure in knowing that the beach is "well-patrolled." We presume that people who come to the beach "looking for trouble" would, unlike beachgoers, make it their business to look out for the police. If this is so, then they would be likely to see Unit 99 and might, as a consequence, think twice about risking criminal activities. Police patrols on the beach may also deter crime by increasing the likelihood of direct police observation of criminal activity. Thus persons about to engage in a crime may be forced by the arrival of a police officer to break off the act or be arrested. Finally, it is possible that the presence of police on the beach may become known to persons who might otherwise look upon the beach as an easy place to steal or to molest women. Such persons might then go elsewhere in search of safer places to achieve their goals. Of course, this conjecture depends upon the assumption that persons who commit crimes at the beach would be constrained by the probability of police detection. Confirmation of this assumption would require research with persons who have either committed or contemplated criminal activity at the beach.

Unfortunately, it was only possible to interview six men who admitted that they had engaged in criminal activities on Southland Beach.[2] All said that they watched carefully for the police and avoided misconduct whenever the police were nearby. For example, a middle-class Anglo man in his fifties admitted that he "used to" expose himself to young women on Southland Beach. Although he often engaged in such behavior, he was very cautious to do so out of the sight of lifeguards, and he monitored the progress of Unit 99 to be certain that it was nowhere nearby. He added that although he had exposed himself to women "hundreds of times," no one had ever complained to the police about him.

Four Anglo men who admitted to being thieves on Southland Beach were also interviewed. All emphasized that they looked very carefully for the police before stealing anything.

Two were teenagers who stole on this beach regularly during the summers; both had been arrested and now stole elsewhere because they felt that the police on Southland Beach could recognize them. Two older men who "used to be" thieves on a more selective basis had never been arrested. All of these men felt that police presence on Southland Beach deterred crime.

The only person interviewed who expressed anything but respect for the deterring effect of police presence was a young Chicano street gang member; he said, like the others, that gang members try to avoid the police, if possible, but added that if he were apprehended by the police in criminal activities (usually gang fights), that it would be important for him to stand up to the police "like a man." Thus while he and his fellow gang members would try to avoid detection by the police, they might, if detected, worsen the trouble by confronting or assaulting the investigating officer. Although he did not say so directly, he implied that some members of his gang might even seek a confrontation with the police in order to demonstrate their courage. The reports of six self-confessed criminals can hardly be conclusive, but they do suggest the possibility that criminals are aware of police patrol on the beach, and of undercover police officers,[3] even if ordinary beachgoers are not.

In the absence of conclusive direct evidence for police deterrence of crime, we must turn to indirect evidence, such as the relationship between crime reports and increased patrol activity. As we have seen, prior to the summer of 1974 when the regular patrol by Unit 99 was instituted, police officers rarely had a visible presence on the beach. After Unit 99 became a reality, there was not only a visible police presence on the beach, but the balloon-tired, four-wheel-drive vehicle and the "beach uniform" of the officer made rapid response possible and foot pursuit effective. If police presence does serve to reduce criminal activity, we would expect that the effect of Unit 99 would be to reduce crime at the beach (obviously, it was the hope of the SCPD that establishing Unit 99 would have this effect). The available evidence that bears upon this effect is not entirely satisfactory, since records in some years were incomplete, and those for others were inaccessible. The best available evidence comes from police crime reports. Every report of a misdemeanor or a felony is placed in this file whether or not a suspect is cited or arrested. It is possible to compare such crime reports for July, August, and September of 1972 (a period for which complete records are available) with crime reports for the same period in 1974, 1975, and 1976.

If visible police presence and rapid response time reduces crime, we would expect to find relatively more crime reports filed in 1972, when police patrol was less efficient in deterring or apprehending crime. Officers in 1972 often could not reach the beach in time to apprehend a suspect or to question a victim. Under these conditions, we assume that more crimes were committed (and reported) because the chance of detection was slight. Unit 99 began its patrol activity during the last few days of June 1974. Its patrols in July 1974 were somewhat unpredictable, because of a shortage of patrol officers and a police practice of calling Unit 99 off the beach to deal with crime elsewhere in the city. Nevertheless, Unit 99 made at least a short beach patrol almost every day in July 1974. We would expect that these patrols would *increase* the number of crime reports because officers could now surprise offenders before they were able to escape and because they could now reach victims in time to question them and thus file a crime report. On the other hand, we would expect that the visual deterrent effect of Unit 99 would not yet have taken place. Because patrols by Unit 99 were more frequent and more regular in August and September 1974, we would expect a deterrent effect to begin, leading to fewer crime reports compared to the same months in 1972. Patrols by Unit 99 continued throughout the remainder of 1974, as well as 1975 and 1976. By the summer of 1975 we would expect to find a still greater reduction in crime reports, since persons who were able to commit crimes with relative impunity in 1972 would by now realize that they were running a high risk of detection by the police.

Table 5 provides the data necessary to examine these expectations. It appears that the expected pattern of crime reports did in fact take place, at least until 1976. Thus in July 1974, the first months of Unit 99's activities, there were 106 crime reports compared to only 67 reports for the entire month of July in 1972—an increase of 38 percent. As the summer wore on, it would appear that Unit 99 began to have the predicted deterrent effect, with the result that there were fewer crime reports in August (by 32 percent) and in September (by 36 percent) than in the same months of 1972. The reduction in 1975 compared to 1972 was still more dramatic. As predicted, there was also a reduction in crime reports from 1974 to 1975. However, while July of 1976 continued this trend of reduced crime reports, both August and September of 1976 showed an increase over the same months in 1975. We cannot explain this increase.

The figures in Table 5 represent all crime reports regardless of the time of day. There was a similarly large reduction of crime reports during the peak crowding hours of 10 A.M. to 4 P.M., with 61 such reports in 1972, 74 in 1974 (45 of which occurred in July), 38 in 1975, and 43 in 1976. We should note that this reduction took place over a period of time when crime in Southland City was increasing.[4] It should also be noted that there were no statistically significant differences

### Table 5
Beach Crime Reports for the Summers
of 1972, 1974, 1975, and 1976
(showing percentage increase or decrease from 1972)

| Month | 1972 | 1974 | 1975 | 1976 |
|-------|------|------|------|------|
| July | 67 reports | 106 reports | 51 reports | 34 reports |
| | | 37% increase | 24% decrease | 49% decrease |
| Aug. | 72 reports | 49 reports | 34 reports | 53 reports |
| | | 32% decrease | 53% decrease | 26% decrease |
| Sept. | 44 reports | 28 reports | 17 reports | 27 reports |
| | | 36% decrease | 61% decrease | 39% decrease |

between the years in terms of the types of crimes reported. The same type of crimes were reported in all four years; it is simply that there were more of them in 1972 and in July of 1974.

It must be emphasized that this evidence is only suggestive, but it seems to confirm what experienced lifeguards and most police officers told us—namely, that Unit 99 has been successful in reducing the occurrence of crime at Southland Beach, and that it is certainly likely that the lifeguard-police network plays a significant part in holding down the frequency of serious trouble on this beach. However, a great many factors that could be related to these changes in the frequency of crime reports were not controlled. For example, beachgoers may have "mellowed" since 1972, as some lifeguards believe. Economic changes may have put fewer transients on the beach. Less restrictive policing practices on other beaches may have attracted troublemakers away from Southland Beach. The rise in crime reports in July 1974 might in part have been due to police zealousness to justify a new and expensive patrol unit; in subsequent months, police officers may have felt less need to file crime reports. As recently as 1976, many local factors may have influenced the crime rates. For example, two of the delapidated apartment buildings that previously housed transients and others who committed crimes were remodeled, and became decidedly high-rent and middle-class buildings. Also, a bike path was constructed all along the sand, making it easier for outsiders to commit crimes and escape rapidly. Further, 1976 was marked by an increase of teenage violence by inner-city gangs, who were apparently unaffected by police visibility or reaction.

Assessing the extent to which police activities deter trouble is at best a perilous business. With enough history to examine, it may be possible to do so with confidence, as in the classic case of London, where a new sort of police organization was able to retrieve the city from the brink of civil chaos (Silver, 1967). Even without such historical depth, there has been some research in the United States that attributes a deterrent effect either to police activity or to harsher penalties.[5] However, most researchers find the evidence unconvincing, or at best difficult to assess (Zimring and Hawkins, 1973).

The evidence from Southland Beach suggests that lifeguards and police officers reduce trouble on the beach primarily by their effects on transients, gang members, or criminals. That they have a similar effect in reducing trouble among ordinary beachgoers is more difficult to demonstrate. For one thing, we must keep in mind that a majority of all the beachgoers we interviewed were not even aware that police officers patrolled the beach. It also seems that trouble among ordinary beachgoers is typically impulsive, not "premeditated," and therefore less likely to be constrained by police presence. To understand the relative absence of trouble among these ordinary beachgoers, it seems necessary to examine more than the actions of lifeguards and police officers.

### Defining the Situation

It was over fifty years ago that sociologist W. I. Thomas stated what was to become an aphorism: "If men define situations as real, they are real in their consequences." Like most aphorisms, this one leaves much unsaid, but it does point dramatically to what has become one of the few indisputable assertions of social science, namely, that how people define situations affects how they behave in them (McHugh, 1968). Thus various social scientists have used concepts such as "situation," "setting," "definition of the situation," "frame," and "culture" to specify the ways in which human behavior is guided by beliefs about what is or what ought to be.

Beachgoers' beliefs—their definitions of the beach situation—were evoked by various kinds of interviews on Southland Beach and elsewhere. These interviews indicated resoundingly that almost all beachgoers, even women alone on the beach, believed that the beach was fun and that it was

safe. Many beachgoers, male and female, regular and occasional, were also interviewed in their homes. With a few qualifications, they agreed that this beach is both enjoyable and
safe. Our personal observations on Southland Beach often
confirmed, and only rarely contradicted, that how these
beachgoers acted was consistent with what they said. What
all but a few of these beachgoers said was this: the beach is
relaxing, fun, healthy, beautiful, serene, a bit romantic, or
even erotic, but wholesome for all of that, and safe—safer
than almost any other public place. They believed that this
beach attracts people who want to escape from their problems, hostilities, or conflicts for an afternoon in order to "mellow out." Beachgoers said that Southland Beach is a place to
relax totally, and that such relaxation means adopting a "live
and let live" attitude in which everyone "minds his own business." For these reasons, they say, and because of the
presence of so many relaxed and tolerant people, trouble at
the beach is a rarity. It is left behind. All but about 5 percent of
the people interviewed consistently and convincingly provided this definition of Southland Beach. Only a few said that
there was trouble at this beach, and even these added that
they enjoyed the place so much that they willingly, if warily,
put up with some trouble.

When we asked people how they came to think about the
beach this way, most responded with blank looks of puzzlement. They had never thought about Southland Beach in any
*other* way. Why should they? Many said that they had gone to
this beach as children and had loved it ever since; many referred to some memorably beautiful experience they had had
there. Almost all said that the physical setting itself made
people relax and avoid conflict. People referred to the soft
warm sand, the pleasant breezes, the tranquil sound of the
surf, the clear, smog-free air, the warm sun and lovely tan it
gives, the water, the sky, the palm trees, and most of all a
sense of beauty and restfulness. It was common for them to
insist that it was unthinkable that people would make trouble
for one another in a setting like that.

Only a very few beachgoers could remember hearing anything negative about this beach from friends, family members, or television. Nor had they read anything in the newspapers to indicate that the beach was unsafe. Women sometimes heard about men who bothered other women, and quite a few had heard complaints about litter and crowding, but nothing had accumulated in the lives of these beachgoers to disabuse them of their conviction that Southland Beach is both pleasant and safe.

Like most aspects of culture, it is difficult to retrace the process by which this set of beliefs about Southland Beach grew and took hold, and we made no effort to do the historical work that might clarify the matter. Most beachgoers had gone to this beach for many years, and it is likely that the beach used to be even more pleasant and safe than it is today. Surely, it is so portrayed in movies, television, and popular literature.[6] We do know that beliefs about the safety of this beach are now widespread and firmly held. Thus beachgoers today are provided with firm beliefs and psychological expectations that define the activity of beachgoing. Because these beliefs and expectations define the beach as a place where trouble rarely occurs, it is possible that beachgoers actually fail to perceive certain behaviors as troublesome, and thus by their selective attention to the behavior of others may succeed in "defining" away some of the trouble that does occur on the beach. Surely if a beachgoer truly believes that trouble will not occur, he is not likely to construe ambiguous behavior as troublesome. He is more likely to sink back into his securely relaxed mood, and to ignore whatever might be going on. This sort of inattention to possible trouble often occurs on the beach, and it must help to reaffirm existing beliefs that all is well.

But we also know that in addition to sharing a general definition of the beach situation, beachgoers typically engage in behaviors that seem designed to reduce still further both their realization that trouble is occurring and their display of alarm in reaction to it. Beachgoers also avoid behaviors that might either encourage or exacerbate trouble. These routine behaviors also help to explain why the beach is relatively free of trouble.

### Encapsulation: Routines of Isolation and Non-Involvement

Beachgoers on Southland Beach regularly behave in ways that serve to ignore, avoid, or minimize trouble. Thus, as we have seen, they establish private territories on the sand and with a few exceptions they keep to themselves within these territories. Except for the most innocuous kinds of greetings or requests, beachgoers rarely interact with strangers.[7] Instead they encapsulate themselves against the people around them to such an extent that they often fail to recognize that something is amiss; they "mind their own business" and only rarely take action that would involve them in a troublesome encounter. Finally, if trouble intrudes directly into their private territories they will typically gather up their possessions and move away rather than confront or challenge the troublesome person.

We are tempted to express some measure of surprise concerning the ability of so many undressed people to encapsulate themselves from one another, but a second thought suggests that it may be this very sense of vulnerability or privacy created by being undressed among strangers that makes such isolation necessary, even inevitable. That people have the capacity to isolate themselves from one another almost completely no matter how intimate the circumstances should certainly be no surprise either. Consider that Siamese twins have learned to maintain their individual privacy under the most trying of circumstances, even to the extent that one twin can go on about his or her private and non-sexual business while the other engages in sexual intercourse (Drimmer 1973). Beachgoers cannot go this far, but they can and do ignore instances of lovemaking, sexual exposure, drunkenness, loud radios, argumentation, and even physical conflict taking place only a few sandy yards away. Many analysts have noted that urban Americans regularly create "shields of privacy" against strangers in many public places,[8] so their encapsulation on Southland Beach is hardly unique.

It is also true that many of the routine beach behaviors displayed on Southland Beach parallel behaviors that have been reported for other public places. Thus, for example, Erving Goffman's many writings about public behavior are frequently relevant to this beach. His concepts about kinds of social occasions are often apt, as for example, his notion that some occasions are "unserious," participated in for the sheer pleasure of doing so (1963:19). The beach is "unserious." Goffman has also tried to typify situations as loose (or informal) versus tight (or formal), and has suggested that unusual attire such as bathing suits may help to make a situation loose and informal. He has contrasted settings with regard to how "open" they are, with an open setting being one—like a bar or a party—in which anyone who enters is expected to make himself or herself accessible to anyone else in the vicinity (1963:134). The beach is clearly not an "open" setting. People at the beach are "inaccessible" and "uninvolved," two other concepts that Goffman has elaborated. His many discussions of "territories of the self" (1971) can also be applied to beach behavior with profit, as we have already noted. So it is with his ideas on "alarms," "normal appearances," and sense of vulnerability (1971).

There are too many other parallels between Goffman's views of public behavior and what we have seen on the beach to mention them all here, but one last concept deserves attention. Goffman coined the term "civil inattention," which he described as follows: "What seems to be involved is that one gives to another enough visual notice to demonstrate that one appreciates that the other is present (and that one admits openly to seeing him), while at the next moment withdrawing one's attention from him so as to express that he does not constitute a target of special curiosity or design" (1963:84). This description sometimes fits the visual attention, or inattention, that occurs between male beachgoers or between groups who meet at the beach, especially when walking onto or away from the sand; more often, however, even this degree of visual recognition is lacking. Women, especially lone women, typically avoid even the minimal recognition involved in "civil inattention." The beach does not seem to be a place where one must "give notice;" one establishes a private territory and isolates oneself. Others need not be recognized or disarmed by visual contact.

Stanley Milgram (1970) has called attention to what he believes are typical, perhaps essential, features of urban living. Much of his argument relates to the effect that sensory overload in large cities has had in causing people to conserve their psychic energy by disregarding low priority inputs in favor of a limited number of high priority phenomena. Whether overload is in fact the operative mechanism is not at issue here. What does concern us are the adaptive responses to urban conditions (large numbers, density, and heterogeneity) that Milgram identifies. He believes that urban dwellers share an attitude or value that says "don't meddle" as well as an affectively laden attitude of personal vulnerability. These attitudes or values lead city people to tolerate strangers at the same time that they fear them. It is possible to interpret beach behavior in these terms. Beachgoers do not meddle and some women at least do feel vulnerable. Although most beachgoers explicitly deny that they fear strangers at the beach, their actions suggest that while they may trust beachgoers whose appearances are normal, they may fear those who do not appear to be ordinary beachgoers like themselves.

A more explicit set of "adaptive" behaviors has been proposed by Lyn Lofland (1973:151–55) in her study of strangers' interactions in urban public places. She believes that strangers in public attempt to maintain "symbolic shields of privacy" by adhering to the following principles: (1) "minimize expressivity"—facial expressions, laughter, tears, singing, and talking should all be avoided; (2) "minimize body contact"—avoid bumping into, brushing past, or otherwise touching strangers; (3) "look before you sit"—avoid suggesting to a stranger that one wishes to interact; (4) "minimize eye contact"—avoid even accidental eye contact; (5) "when in doubt, flee"—avoid coming near to anyone who looks odd or behaves strangely, and if accosted, flee; (6) "when in doubt, disattend"—if it is impossible to flee, pay no attention, thereby doing nothing to suggest that the stranger is in any way not "normal" and therefore dangerous. While the first of Lofland's principles does not apply at the beach, the others certainly do, suggesting that, especially for women, Southland Beach is by no means a unique public setting. However, even for lone women, the beach would appear to be a place that is far less tense, more trusting and more comfortable, than the urban places Lofland discusses. Almost all of the women we interviewed made it quite clear that they were far more trusting and comfortable at the beach than they would be in a bar or on a bus, not to mention truly frightening places like dark streets or parking buildings.

In reviewing the implications of this research on an urban beach, there is a final, and fundamental, issue to consider. That issue concerns the role of what can be called "community" versus "individuation" in urban public behavior. As used here, "community" refers to a collectivity of people who feel personal involvement and intimacy for one another, who share a moral and emotional commitment not only to one another but to their way of life, and whose way of life exhibits social cohesion and continuity over time. When these concerns, commitments, and involvements are absent, the result can be referred to as individuation.

Few ideas in social science are more commonplace, or more basic, than the notion that the shift from folk community to urban society and individuation brought with it massive changes in human behavior, principal among which were increased social disorder and deviance (Redfield 1947; Mills 1959). There is, of course, a large body of writing—beginning with Henry Maine, Fustel de Coulanges, Otto von Gierke, Ferdinand Tönnies, Georg Simmel, Emile Durkheim, Herbert Spencer, and Max Weber and continuing to the present day—which elaborates the socially deleterious consequences of this loss of community (Nisbet 1966). So pervasive is this point of view that in modern times it has become almost axiomatic to attribute the ills of urban living more or less directly to the social disorganization which is thought to have resulted from the loss of community (Kaplan 1971). For example, we have already heard from Slater (1970) about the undesirable consequences of individuation in America.

That the role of the loss of community in the creation of social disorganization and deviance may be a misreading of the ethnographic record has only recently become a serious point of view (Edgerton 1976).[9] Nevertheless, we can no longer ignore the high rates of deviance that occur in most small communities throughout the world. For example, the Mayan Indians of the small township of Teklum in Mexico have recorded a murder rate of 250 per 100,000 compared to 4.8 per 100,000 for the United States (Nash 1967). And the Gusii tribesmen of Kenya have a reported rape frequency of 47.2 per 100,000 compared to 13.9 for the urban United States (LeVine 1959). Within the United States itself we know that crime rates can be high even in the rural hinterlands (Gibbons 1972), and we can hardly disregard the fact that nationwide the risk of assault from family members or friends—our most intimate form of community—is twice as great as it is from strangers (President's Commission 1967).

With these cautions in mind, then, we ask whether a sense of community among beachgoers contributes significantly to the maintenance of social order on Southland Beach. There are still beaches in Southern California that are reported to have a strong sense of community. Surfer beaches, "private beaches," and nude beaches all claim such properties. We have made limited observations on beaches such as these, as well as others in Southern California; but without an investment of time and resources comparable to that given the research on Southland Beach, we can only say that such beaches appear to have even less trouble, and that this may be due to the sense of community among beachgoers at these places.[10] For example, Douglas and others (1977:102) report a very low incidence of trouble on the nude beach they studied, saying that they never saw any fights among nude beachgoers and never even heard of a rape. However, we cannot reject the possibility that this apparently low rate of trouble is a result of the relative inaccessibility of such beaches to the kinds of "troublemakers" (transients, criminals, and the like) who are so common on Southland Beach. The nude beach Douglas and his colleagues describe is extremely inaccessible compared to Southland Beach.

Southland Beach itself has only a few collectivities of beachgoers who exhibit any sense of community. The most obvious of these are volleyball players and surfers. Volleyball players do express a strong sense of mutual concern and intimacy; they have clear knowledge of their membership and of the rules and symbols that govern their conduct; they effectively control their own public conduct, and they take collective action against outsiders whose behavior is offensive— they have done so for many years. They have a sense of community in almost every conceivable way. But there are only a handful—perhaps 100—volleyball players on Southland Beach, so their conduct has almost no influence on the hundreds of thousands of ordinary beachgoers who go there each summer day. Surfers, too, have a sense of community which is focused on finding and riding the best possible waves. Surfers on Southland Beach express their collective interests most often in hostile acts toward the lifeguards or beachgoers who thwart their free use of the surf. They have little or nothing to do with ordinary beachgoers, except occasionally to fight with them or steal belongings from their cars.

In the absence of any direct evidence for a sense of community among ordinary beachgoers on Southland Beach, we turn once again to indirect evidence. Most trouble, especially violent trouble, occurs on the South beach area, which is far more accessible than North beach to non-beachgoers who may make trouble. Thus among the many persons who come to stroll fully clothed on the promenade or pier are juvenile gang members, thieves, psychotics, drunks, drug addicts, and sex offenders. Some of these people are drifters with no address, no income, and long police records. Most of the serious crime on South beach is probably committed by these kinds of people who stray onto the beach, not by ordinary beachgoers themselves. Available police records permit no precise count, but it appears that as many as half of the offenses committed in this area can be attributed to fully clothed persons who cannot be considered "beachgoers," and that well over half the violent crime is their doing.[11] Does this mean that there is a sense of community on North beach that controls trouble? Not that we could identify. It seems more reasonable to conclude that South beach is simply more accessible to non-beachgoing troublemakers than North beach is.

In this same regard, we should also note that reported crime at Southland Beach does not increase proportionately to the size of the beach crowd. Our beach observations showed that there was an average of 1.6 rule violations per hour on crowded weekend days, with the average for less crowded weekdays being slightly less than 1.0 per hour (see Chapter Five). However, an examination of police records indicates just the reverse, as Table 6 shows. It is clear that as crowd size increases, the probability of *reported* crime decreases. There are several possible explanations for this phenomenon. First, it is possible that there is a kind of safety in numbers, in the sense that as crowds of people on the beach increase, persons who might otherwise choose to commit crimes are deterred. But our own observations, and our discussions with lifeguards and police officers, suggest that the more likely explanation is that law enforcement becomes increasingly difficult as crowds grow. Due to the numbers of people on the sand, it is almost impossible for guards and police to react quickly. Under such circumstances, it is difficult for the police to detect criminal activity or even to respond to citizens' complaints. We presume, therefore, that the inverse relationship between crowd size and crime reports is largely an artifact of the difficulties of law enforcement. We assume, as our observations indicate, that trouble occurs somewhat more often on crowded days than on uncrowded ones, but that it cannot easily be reported or recorded.

The important point is this: even if there is substantial unreported and unrecorded crime on the most crowded days, order on this beach clearly does not break down. Social con-

**Table 6**

Relationship of Crowd Size to Crime Reports During
Summer Months, 1975, 10 A.M. to 4 P.M.

| Total Crowd Per Day | Days | Total Persons Involved | Total No. of FI's | Ratio of FI to Population | Total No. of Crime Reports | Ratio of Crime Reports to Population |
|---|---|---|---|---|---|---|
| 25,000 or less | 19 | 250,000 | 35 | 1:9,510 | 2 | 1:125,000 |
| 75,000 to 26,000 | 34 | 1,662,000 | 48 | 1:34,625 | 16 | 1:103,875 |
| 150,000 to 76,000 | 29 | 3,538,000 | 40 | 1:88,450 | 14 | 1:252,714 |
| 400,000 to 150,000 | 9 | 2,275,000 | 21 | 1:108,333 | 6 | 1:379,166 |

trol may be less effective on such days, but beachgoers continue their trouble-reducing routines, and their beliefs in the
safety and pleasure of the beach are unchanged. How many
people are together on the beach does not seem to matter,
even though weekends bring to the beach large numbers of
inner-city residents who are unlikely to share any sense of
community with the local beachgoers.

If we are to understand the effect that the absence of a
sense of community plays at Southland Beach, we must understand first of all that beachgoers there are strangers. Like
visitors to many public places—such as zoos or sports events
or movies or elevators, as various beachgoers mentioned—
they share space and even mingle, but they remain strangers.
They do not shake hands and introduce themselves. They do
not exchange names, telephone numbers, or business cards.
They do not talk to one another or play together. When they
leave they rarely see one another again, at the beach or
elsewhere.

The social order we see at the beach, then, is not akin to
what we are familiar with in small communities, or in places
where face-to-face interaction occurs, like parties. Instead,
social order at this beach is more like what is seen at a college
football game attended by 100,000 people who park, sit
together, cheer or groan, and then leave, having made no
lasting contacts with one another. Beachgoing is similar to a
football game because the experience is transitory and impersonal, but it is potentially more personal and more dangerous. At a football game an occasional drunk may become
abusive, a few fans may argue or even exchange punches,
and someone may be mugged on the way out of the stadium,
but the game is the focus of attention for almost everyone.
Indeed, a recent police report indicates that trouble within the
mammoth Los Angeles Coliseum during football games is
neither serious nor common (*Los Angeles Times*, December 4,
1976). At a beach, unlike a football game, there is no such
focus, no sense of start and finish, no clear purpose except
enjoyment of oneself and the elements. No one pays a large
sum for a ticket. Unlike a football game, where everyone is
there for the same purpose, people who come to the beach for

enjoyment are often observed or bothered by persons drawn to the beach like parasites, to look at or prey upon the belongings or the bodies of beachgoers; and there are many, many vulnerable, near-naked bodies lying in the sun. Yet somehow, trouble is controlled or neutralized or evaded, leaving beachgoing as an experience that beachgoers continue to see as safe and pleasant.

This accomplishment—and an accomplishment it assuredly is—seems to be possible precisely because beachgoers do remain strangers. As we have mentioned, there are beaches elsewhere where beachgoers come to know one another and to establish a sense of community with one another. Southland Beach is not such a place. It is a beach that attracts people from all over one of the world's largest metropolitan areas. These people visit this beach for a few hours and return home, expecting to come again when opportunity permits. To borrow Toffler's phrase, the beach experience is one of "temporariness." It would be no simple matter to maintain peaceable interaction among such different kinds of undressed and intoxicated people whose presence on this beach is so transitory. The effort to interact, in fact, would probably produce conflict. Most conflict, especially violent conflict, occurs between friends and relatives, not strangers, especially not strangers who do not interact. Instead of seeing themselves as part of a community, beachgoers on Southland Beach share the idea that they should be left alone to relax and to enjoy their own private world. Beachgoing is an individualized experience. This is not only an inference from beachgoers' behavior; they said so themselves again and again.

Beachgoers are together yet alone, and these two facts give them a measure of safety. The police shield them from outsiders who might victimize them. They shield themselves from one another. It may not be altogether comforting to realize that public safety in an urban place can best be achieved by the isolation of one person from his neighbor. It may be even less comforting to realize that people at Southland Beach find not only safety but pleasure in being alone—together.

Is this individuation a version of the enforced privatization that Riesman and others (1950) discussed in *The Lonely Crowd*? Is it born of fear of others or of distaste for them? Is it merely a preference for solitude in a relaxing ambiance? Is it a desire for loneliness? Some will no doubt be tempted to see Southland Beach as a fulfillment of Colin Turnbull's (1972) apocalyptic vision of the Ik, who sat alone together, not speaking, while they slowly starved to death and their culture lost its last vestiges of sociability.

Interpretations of this sort may appeal to the more pessimistic among us, but such interpretations should not be accepted uncritically. For one thing, we cannot assume that all beachgoers have the same reasons for encapsulating themselves on the beach. Indeed, not all do so, because some single people are willing to meet others on Southland Beach. Furthermore, it is important to recognize that there is much sociability on Southland Beach; it is simply restricted to persons who come to the beach together. That urban Americans who are visiting a recreational setting with friends or family should avoid interaction with strangers is hardly surprising. More than 80 percent of all beachgoers on Southland Beach go there with someone else with whom they interact in various, usually happy, ways. Thus 80 percent of the persons on Southland Beach are not alone, nor do they appear to be lonely. They are with someone of their choice.

Just why beachgoers avoid strangers is not the question this research set out to answer. The attempt to disinter motivation has been a dubious enterprise at least since Mills (1940) wrote about the rhetoric of motives, and it has become nearly unthinkable since the writings of Peters (1958). The question here is not why beachgoers behave as they do, although their own answers to this question have been presented. The question here is, what allows strangers on Southland Beach to get along together? It seems indisputable that their private encapsulation, which restricts interaction among strangers to an absolute minimum, is an important means by which potential conflict is avoided, and relaxed pleasure is achieved. "Community," as we ordinarily understand it, seems to have little to do with the achievement of social order on Southland

Beach; however, a kind of "natural identity of interests"—the tacit agreement that beachgoers should be left alone to relax—appears to have a great deal to do with social order there. But whatever we call this—privatization, encapsulation, or individuation—it is different from a sense of community. Beachgoing is an individualized experience, not a collective one. Yet social theorists who have seen the loss of community and the advent of individuation as the root cause of social disorder or deviance, or of personal aberration, loneliness or insecurity, will find little support for their perspective from Southland Beach. On this beach, individuation seems to contribute not only to the maintenance of social order but to the experience of pleasure and security as well.

We began this study by recalling the classic antinomy between Hobbes and Locke, the former attributing social order to social control, the latter to a natural identity of interests. We can now see that social order at this urban beach cannot be understood solely in terms of one point of view or the other. Neither is it simply a product of the two. The relatively trouble-free social order that exists among beachgoers at Southland Beach depends on a common definition of the beach situation as well as a shared set of routine behaviors. These two factors are effective in suppressing serious trouble among actual beachgoers. A third factor, the presence of lifeguard and police protection, restricts trouble still further, especially by defending beachgoers against the fully clothed outsiders who might otherwise victimize them.

Because of the limitations of this study, these conclusions must be offered tentatively, with all of the caveats so characteristic of the social sciences. We cannot demonstrate to the complete satisfaction of even the least skeptical that all three factors are in fact essential to the maintenance of order on Southland Beach. Much less can we show exactly how each factor operates as it does. That is the curse—and for the public, whom we study, perhaps the blessing—of naturalistic methodology in the social sciences. We cannot, for example, experiment by removing all lifeguards and police officers from the beach while we record changes in the amount and kind of trouble that follows. But if we could, we would predict that serious crime would increase greatly, making pleasant and safe beachgoing a virtual impossibility. As one former thief at Southland Beach put it, "Man, if the cops weren't here this place would be wild. I think even I'd be afraid to come here." Nor can we change the definition of the beach situation—for example, by mounting a multi-media campaign to convince the public of the dangers at Southland Beach. But if we were to do so, by promoting a definition of the situation like that held by people in New York about the subway (Levine and others 1973) or Central Park at night, we would again predict that Southland Beach could not long remain a relatively orderly and trouble-free place. That is so because there are enough strange and menacing people on this beach to alarm anyone who might go there thinking of it as a dangerous place and of themselves as in need of protection. Finally, we cannot alter beachgoers' routines, by encouraging them to interact with strangers or to intervene when these strangers seem to be in conflict; but if such changes were to occur, we would again predict that even with the police on duty and a positive definition of the beach in effect, trouble would quickly become both much more common and much more serious. That is so because strangers at Southland Beach are so diverse that interaction among them could hardly fail to bring about misunderstanding, and where age and cultural differences are so great, efforts to mediate conflict would seem likely to fail more often than not.

To paraphrase Hobbes' question about the problem of order, can people who are left to themselves get along with one another? As far as Southland Beach is concerned the answer is yes—*if* people are literally left to themselves, *if* they think of themselves as safe, and *if* they are watched over by the police. While this answer might not please either Hobbes or Locke, it seems likely that it applies not only to Southland Beach but to many of our urban places.

# Appendix:
# Research Procedures

Systematic research on Southland Beach began in June 1975. The initial procedures were ethnographic ones designed to produce a portrait of customary as well as unusual beach activities. These ethnographic approaches relied primarily on participant-observation, because this beach is a setting where one can quickly become as authentic a beachgoer as almost anyone else. Moreover, the author was able to draw upon personal knowledge of Southland Beach; in the late 1940s, as a high school student, he was an occasional beachgoer there, and he has often lived near this beach or visited it since. Most of the research assistants who joined in this study also had years of prior experience there. Ethnographic research continued throughout all of 1976 and part of 1977. Systematic observation and interviewing was carried out primarily in the summer months of 1975 and 1976, with some additional research being done in 1977. Lifeguard and police records and activities were examined throughout 1975 and 1976. Some comparative research on other kinds of beaches in Southern California was also begun in 1976 and carried on into 1977. Details of these various research procedures have been provided at appropriate places throughout the text.

A word of caution is necessary. While it was possible to observe the public behavior of all kinds of beachgoers on Southland Beach, it was not possible to interview all of these beachgoers with equal ease. We did talk to people from the ages of 13 to over 70, both male and female, on all parts of the beach. English-speaking Asians, blacks, and whites were interviewed more-or-less in proportion to their numbers, but Spanish-speaking beachgoers were under-represented in interviews because of the language barrier (and sometimes their reluctance to be interviewed at all).

## Interview Schedule for Women Without Male Escorts

Day of Week or Date
Time of Day
Weather
Age
Beach Location
Marital Status

1. How often do you come to the beach?
2. How long do you stay?
3. For how many years have you been coming to this beach?
4. Where do you live?
5. What is your favorite part of the beach?
6. What do you like most about the beach?
7. Do you swim?
8. Do you ever come early or late in the day?
9. Do you generally talk to other people or do you stay pretty much to yourself?
10. Have you ever made a friend at the beach?
11. Do you ever talk to strangers?
12. Do strangers ever talk to you? (How do you feel about that?)
13. Has anything really nice or special ever happened to you at the beach?
14. Has anything really unpleasant happened?
15. Is there anything that annoys you here?
16. If something happened that really upset you, what would you do?
17. What would you do if: (a) Something of yours were stolen?
                              (b) You needed first aid?
                              (c) You saw a man exposing himself, or something like that?

18. Do you remember seeing anyone whose appearance or behavior on the beach bothered you?
19. Since we're all strangers at the beach, really, why do you think it is possible for us to get along together?
20. What would you like to change about the beach to make it a more enjoyable place?

Notes: (Physical description, comments, etc.)

# Notes

## Chapter 1

1. For an anthropological discussion of the problem of order, see Colson (1974). For a more general view, see Douglas (1971), Gouldner (1970), Wrong (1961), Lyman and Scott (1970), and Scott (1972). For an instructive historical account of order and change in a nineteenth-century American town undergoing urbanization, see Blumin (1976).

2. For a discussion of these traditions, see Zeitlin (1973).

3. In this regard, I have been particularly influenced by the work of Matza (1969), Colson (1974), Cancian (1975), Bailey (1969), Douglas (1973), Gluckman (1972), Black (1976), Schutz (1967), Garfinkel (1967), Spradley (1970), and, of course, Goffman (1963, 1967, 1971, 1974).

## Chapter 2

1. This large pier is a dramatically different setting from the beach area around it. Cars may drive on the pier, and most visitors to it are fully dressed. Activities on the pier itself were not studied systematically, and these activities are excluded from consideration in this book.

2. A paved bikeway was built along the sandy beach on South beach in 1976. Although this bikeway extends onto North beach, there it is located at the rear of the beach, not out on the sand itself, as is the case on South beach.

3. In 1976 two of these apartments were renovated so extensively that they became moderately priced.

4. Some information on the world of surfers on a different beach in Southern California is available in Irwin (1973).

5. Quaalude (methaqualone) is a non-barbiturate sedative which, like "reds" or other "downers," can be used to produce a "high" (Bridge and Ellinwood 1973). They are available by prescription only, and were selling at Southland Beach for $2.00 or $2.50 for a single capsule in 1976.

## Chapter 4

1. There are many discussions of such discretion; for example, see Bittner (1967), Potholm and Morgan (1976), Skolnick (1975), and Wilson (1968).

2. There is room in Unit 99 for only two persons (besides prisoners, who may be transported in the caged rear portion of the vehicle). For this reason, only one observer at a time was able to ride in Unit 99. However, both observers were able to accompany the same officers on several occasions.

## Chapter 5

1. Because we were able to draw upon many years of previous experience on this beach, it was possible to complete this preliminary description in only two months.

2. Given the reactivity of so many of the research procedures used in social science, it is worth emphasizing that the observations made on this beach appeared to be completely nonreactive.

3. We did sometimes talk to lifeguards, but this was often not possible because at the time of the event they were often too busy to talk, and the next day they might be assigned to a tower two miles away.

## Chapter 6

1. See Goffman (1971) for a discussion of normal appearances, alarms, and vulnerability.

## Chapter 7

1. Sampling in public places was non-probabilistic; we tried to interview everyone in the setting during a given period, but some persons (about 15 percent) were unwilling to talk. The door-to-door interviews were based on taking every third residence on a randomly selected street until 20 adult respondents had been obtained; if no one was at home in a selected household, the interviewers moved along the street to the next designated residence. The questionnaires with university students were given to all students in various social science classes.

2. No formal sampling procedure was followed. The instructions were simply to interview a diversity of beachgoers at all areas of the beach.

3. The interview schedule is presented in the Appendix.

4. The beach areas sampled were tower numbers 15 and 16 (the heterogeneous areas thought to be more troublesome), towers 8–11, 24–27, and County Beach (the more homogeneous areas of which were thought to be less troublesome).

5. Willoughby and Inciardi (1975) estimate that the ratio of unreported crime in Los Angeles is 2.9:1. Our observations and the beliefs of the SCPD agree that this estimate is far too low where Southland Beach is concerned.

6. Because some of these crime reports referred to persons who had not yet been arrested or tried, it was not possible for us to examine the complete reports. Instead, a card summarizing the essential facts of the crime was made available. Due to a change in police personnel and in recording procedures, the rape statistics for 1976 are not fully comparable to those for previous years.

7. These estimates are subject to change from day to day, and, of course, from area to area on the beach.

## Chapter 8

1. The size of this private territory varies somewhat depending on conditions, such as crowding. On very crowded days, for example, people set up their towels closer to one another than they do when the beach is sparsely crowded. Ethnicity matters also, as Chicanos typically set up their territories closer to others than Anglos do. Ashcraft and Scheffler (1976:18) report that this practice is typical of "hispanic" peoples. For a discussion of spatial invasion, see also Schneiderman and Ewens (1971) and Fisher and Byrne (1975). For a general discussion of Territory, see Hinde (1972).

2. These undergraduate students filled out a questionnaire about their experiences on the beach.

3. In addition to Goffman's (1971) writings about alarms, there is a related literature on interpersonal trust. For a review, see Conviser (1973). For a discussion of privacy, see Schwartz (1968).

4. Confrontation avoidance is common throughout the non-Western world, where fear of retaliation is especially great (Colson 1974). For a case study in a modern Hawaiian population, see Howard (1974).

## Chapter 9

1. Schutz (1967).

2. The responses of the 51 women interviewed at length were in

essential agreement with those of these 66 women, as were those of the 41 lone women interviewed on the beach in 1976.

## Chapter 10

1. Violence on the pier is another story. Daytime violence there can be serious, as witness the fate of a tourist who was attacked with a broken beer bottle, receiving facial cuts so severe that 100 stitches were required to close them.

2. These self-confessed criminals were identified through various contacts, which included local residents, lifeguards, and police officers. Of those identified, only these six were willing to give candid interviews.

3. The SCPD rarely used undercover officers during the period of this research. When such officers were used they were deployed for brief periods only, and with particular criminal activity in mind, such as narcotics sales and homosexual crime. Undercover officers are used primarily at night and on the pier.

4. In the *FBI Uniform Crime Reports for the United States*, U.S. Department of Justice, for the years 1972 through 1976, Southland City (a pseudonym) records a major increase in its overall crime index.

5. See, for example, Bahn (1975), Bankston and Cramer (1974), Becker and Landes (1974), Swimmer (1974), and especially Ehrlich (1975) for his econometric analysis that purports to show that every instance of capital punishment deters 17 homicides.

6. Compare *Gidget* (Kohner 1957) with *Lifeguard* (Racina 1976).

7. Women on the beach without men are a partial exception.

8. See Goffman (1963, 1971), Lofland (1973), Ashcraft and Schefflen (1976), Mehrabian (1976), and Birenbaum and Sagarin (1973).

9. See also Matza (1969), Colson (1974).

10. There are few legally private beaches in Southern California, but there are several sizable beaches that have no convenient public access; these beaches are used almost exclusively by people whose residences front the sand, effectively screening out nonresidents.

11. SCPD crime records often note transients because they can give no address, and these records will occasionally refer to an offender's criminal record if known and to their dress. But because these records are unreliable in all these respects, we can only make estimates based on the records and the memories of lifeguards and police officers. For a discussion of witness cooperation and its relationship to crime reports, see Cannavale and Falcon (1976).

# References

Ashcraft, N., and A. E. Schefflen. *People Space: The Making and Breaking of Human Boundaries.* Garden City, N.Y.: Anchor Books, Doubleday, 1976.

Bailey, F. G. *Stratagems and Spoils: A Social Anthropology of Politics.* Oxford: Blackwell, 1969.

Bahn, C. "The Reassurance Factor in Police Patrol." *Criminology,* 12:338–345, 1974.

Bankston, W. B., and J. A. Cramer. "Toward a Macro-Sociological Interpretation of General Deterrence." *Criminology,* 12:251–280, 1974.

Becker, G. S., and W. M. Landes, eds. *Essays in the Economics of Crime and Punishment.* New York: Columbia University Press, 1974.

Bettman, O. L. *The Good Old Days—They Were Terrible!* New York: Random House, 1974.

Birenbaum, A., and E. Sagarin. *People in Places: The Sociology of the Familiar.* New York: Praeger, 1973.

Bittner, E. "The Police on Skid Row." *American Sociological Review,* 32:699–715, 1967.

Black, D. *The Behavior of Law.* New York: Academic Press, 1976.

Blumin, S. M. *The Urban Threshold: Growth and Change in a Nineteenth-Century Community.* Chicago: University of Chicago Press, 1976.

Bridge, P. T., and E. H. Ellinwood, Jr. "Quaalude Alley: A One Way Street." *American Journal of Psychiatry,* 130:217–219, 1973.

Cancian, F. *What are Norms? A Study of Beliefs and Action in a Maya Community*. London: Cambridge University Press, 1975.

Cannavale, F. J., Jr., and W. D. Falcon, eds. *Witness Cooperation*. Lexington, Mass.: D. C. Heath, 1976.

Cavan, S. *Liquor License: An Ethnography of Bar Behavior*. Chicago: Aldine, 1966.

Colson, E. *Tradition and Contract: The Problem of Order*. Chicago: Aldine, 1974.

Conviser, R. H. "Toward a Theory of Interpersonal Trust." *Pacific Sociological Review*, 16:377–399, 1973.

Cornwell, D. A. "The Management of Tensions Between Conflicting Usages of a Public Place." *The Sociological Review*, 21:197–210, 1973.

Denzin, N. K. "The Logic of Naturalistic Inquiry." *Social Forces*, 50:166–182, 1971.

Douglas, J. D., ed. *Understanding Everyday Life: Toward the Reconstruction of Sociological Knowledge*. London: Routledge and Kegan, Paul, 1971.

Douglas, J. D., P. K. Rasmussen, with C. A. Flanagan. *The Nude Beach*. Beverly Hills, Calif.: Sage, 1977.

Douglas, M. *Purity and Danger: An Analysis of Concepts of Pollution and Taboo*. New York: Praeger, 1966.

Douglas, M., ed. *Rules and Meanings*. London: Penguin, 1973.

Drimmer, F. *Very Special People*. New York: Amjon, 1973.

Edgerton, R. B. *Deviance: A Cross-Cultural Perspective*. Reading, Mass.: Cummings Publishing Co., 1976.

Edney, J. J., and N. L. Jordan-Edney. "Territorial Spacing on a Beach." *Sociometry*, 37:92–104, 1974.

Ehrlich, I. "The Deterrent Effect of Capital Punishment: A Question of Life and Death." *The American Economic Review*, 65:397–417, 1975.

Emerson, J. P. "'Nothing Unusual Is Happening.'" In Tamotsu Shibutani, ed., *Human Nature and Collective Behavior*. Englewood Cliffs, N.J.: Prentice-Hall, 1970.

Fisher, J. D., and D. Byrne. "Too Close for Comfort: Sex Differences in Response to Invasions of Personal Space." *Journal of Personality and Social Psychology*, 32:15–21, 1975.

Gibbons, D. C. "Crime in the Hinterland." *Criminology*, 10:177–191, 1972.

Gibbs, J. P. "Sanctions." *Social Problems*, 14:147–158, 1966.

Goffman, E. *Behavior in Public Places*. New York: The Free Press, 1963.

———. *Interaction Ritual: Essays on Face to Face Behavior*. New York: Doubleday, 1967.

————. *Relations in Public*. New York: Harper and Row, 1971.

————. *Frame Analysis*. New York: Harper and Row, 1974.

Gouldner, A. *The Coming Crisis of Western Sociology*. New York: Basic Books, 1970.

Hinde, R., ed. *Non-verbal Communication*. Cambridge: Cambridge University Press, 1972.

Howard, A. *Ain't No Big Thing: Coping Strategies in a Hawaiian-American Community*. Honolulu: The University of Hawaii Press, 1974.

Irwin, J. "Surfing: The Natural History of an Urban Scene." *Urban Life and Culture*, 2:131–160, 1973.

Kaplan, B. H. *Psychiatric Disorder and the Urban Environment*. New York: Behavioral Publications, 1971.

Kohner, F. *Gidget*. New York: Putnam's, 1957.

Latané, B., and J. M. Darley. *The Unresponsive Bystander: Why Doesn't He Help?* New York: Appleton-Century-Crofts, 1970.

Lejeune, R., and N. Alex. "On Being Mugged: The Event and its Aftermath." *Urban Life and Culture*, 2:259–287, 1973.

LeVine, R. A. "Gusii Sex Offenses: A Study in Social Control." *American Anthropologist*, 61:965–990, 1959.

Levine, J., A. Vinson, and D. Wood. "Subway Behavior." In A. Birenbaum and E. Sagarin, eds., *People in Places: The Sociology of the Familiar*, pp. 208–236. New York: Praeger, 1973.

Lofland, L. H. *A World of Strangers. Order and Action in Urban Public Space*. New York: Basic Books, 1973.

Love, R. L. "The Fountains of Urban Life." *Urban Life and Culture*, 2:161–210, 1973.

Lyman, S. M., and M. B. Scott. *A Sociology of the Absurd*. New York: Appleton-Century-Crofts, 1970.

McHugh, P. *Defining the Situation: The Organization of Meaning in Social Interaction*. Indianapolis: Bobbs-Merrill, 1968.

Matza, D. *Becoming Deviant*. Englewood Cliffs. N.J.: Prentice-Hall, 1969.

Mehrabian, A. *Public Places and Private Spaces. The Psychology of Work, Play, and Living Environments*. New York: Basic Books, 1976.

Milgram, S. "The Experience of Living in Cities." *Science*, 167:1461–1468, 1970.

Mills, C. W. "Situated Action and the Vocabulary of Motives." *American Sociological Review*, 6:904–913, 1940.

————. *The Sociological Imagination*. New York: Oxford University Press, 1959.

Nash, J. "Death as A Way of Life: The Increasing Resort to Homicide in a Maya Indian Community." *American Anthropologist*, 69:455–470, 1967.

Peters, R. S. *The Concept of Motivation*. London: Routledge and Kegan, Paul, 1958.

Phillips, D. L. *Abandoning Method*. San Francisco: Jossey-Bass, 1973.

Potholm, C. P., and R. E. Morgan. *Focus on Police: Police In American Society*. New York: Wiley, 1976.

U.S. President's Commission on Law Enforcement and Administration of Justice Task Force Report, *The Challenge of Crime in a Free Society*. Washington, D.C.: U.S. Government Printing Office, 1967.

Racina, T. *Lifeguard*. New York: Warner Books, 1976.

Redfield, R. "The Folk Society." *American Journal of Sociology*, 52:293–308, 1947.

Riesman, D., with R. Denney and N. Glazer. *The Lonely Crowd*. New Haven: Yale University Press, 1950.

Schneiderman, J. H., and W. L. Ewens. "The Cognitive Effects of Spatial Invasion." *Pacific Sociological Review*, 13:469–486, 1971.

Schutz, A. *The Problem of Social Reality*. Collected Papers, Vol. 1. The Hague: Martinns Nijhoff, 1967.

Schwartz, B. "The Social Psychology of Privacy." *American Journal of Sociology*, 73:741–752, 1968.

Scott, R. A. "A Proposed Framework for Analyzing Deviance as a Property of Social Order." In Robert A. Scott and Jack Douglas, eds., *Theoretical Perspectives on Deviance*. New York: Basic Books, 1972.

Silver, A. "The Demand for Order in Civil Society: A Review of Some Themes in the History of Urban Crime, Police and Riot." In David J. Bordua, ed., *The Police: Six Sociological Essays*, pp. 1–24. New York: John Wiley and Sons, 1967.

Skolnick, J. H. *Justice Without Trial: Law Enforcement in Democratic Society*. 2nd Edition. New York: Wiley, 1975.

Slater, P. *The Pursuit of Loneliness: American Culture at the Breaking Point*. Boston: Beacon Press, 1970.

Spradley, J. *You Owe Yourself A Drunk*. Boston: Little Brown, 1970.

Swimmer, G. "The Relationship of Police and Crime: Some Methodological and Empirical Results." *Criminology*, 12:293–314, 1974.

Toffler, A. *Future Shock*. New York: Random House, 1970.

Turnbull, C. *The Mountain People*. New York: Simon and Schuster, 1972.

Willoughby, E. L., and J. A. Inciardi. "Estimating the Incidence of Crime." *The Police Chief*, 42:69–70, 1975.

Wilson, J. Q. *Varieties of Police Behavior: The Management of Law and Order in Eight Communities*. Cambridge, Mass.: Harvard University Press, 1968.

Wirth, L. "Urbanism as a Way of Life." *The American Journal of Sociology,* 44:1–24, 1938.

Wrong, D. "The Oversocialized Conception of Man in Modern Sociology." *American Sociological Review,* 26:183–193, 1961.

Zeitlin, I. M. *Rethinking Sociology: A Critique of Contemporary Theory.* New York: Appleton-Century-Crofts, 1973.

Zimring, F. E., and G. J. Hawkins. *Deterrence: The Legal Threat in Crime Control.* Chicago: University of Chicago Press, 1973.